TOM and JERRY

PATRICK BRION

TOM and JERRY

THE DEFINITIVE GUIDE
TO THEIR ANIMATED ADVENTURES

Harmony Books/New York

Published by Harmony Books,
a division of Crown Publishers, Inc.,
201 East 50th Street, New York, New York 10022

Originally published in France as TOM ET JERRY
by Patrick Brion in 1987.
Published by Éditions du Chêne.
Copyright © 1987 by Sté Nlle des Éditions du Chêne.
Copyright © 1987 by Turner Entertainment Co.
All rights reserved.
All material reproduced with permission of
Turner Entertainment Co.

HARMONY and colophon are trademarks of Crown Publishers, Inc.

Library of Congress Cataloging-in-Publication Data
Brion, Patrick.
[Tom et Jerry. English]
Tom and Jerry: the definitive guide to
their animated adventures/by Patrick Brion;
translated by Annette Michelson.

Translation of: Tom et Jerry.
1. Tom and Jerry films—History and criticism.
2. Animated films—California—Los Angeles—History and criticism.
I. Title.   II. Title: Tom and Jerry.
PN1997.5.B7513   1990   791.43′651—dc20   89-26825   CIP
ISBN 0-517-57351-2
Printed in Italy - Litho 800 - 20083 Gaggiano - Milano

10   9   8   7   6   5   4   3   2   1
First American Edition

THE ADVENTURES OF TOM AND JERRY

"Hollywood characters are supposed to have all the adventures for everybody in America, while everybody in America sits in a dark room and watches them have them."—Tennessee Williams, *The Glass Menagerie* (1945)

THE GLASS MENAGERIE

In the world of animated film, the partnership of Tom and Jerry has a special claim to eminence. Tom is unquestionably the best-known cat, beating out Sylvester, Tweety Pie's oft-defeated enemy, by several lengths, and Jerry, Tom's faithful tormentor, is unrivaled in his diabolical ingenuity.

For twenty-seven years, from 1940 to 1967, Tom and Jerry's adventures accompanied some of MGM's finest films. This prestigious series, with its wealth of 161 titles, divides into three periods:

> 1940–1957: William Hanna and Joseph Barbera
> 1960–1962: Gene Deitch
> 1963–1967: Chuck Jones

While the last two periods occurred during the decline of the American animated cartoon, the first seventeen years of production represent dazzling artistic genius, inseparable from many of Hollywood's feature-film triumphs.

As we remember the finest hours of Tom and Jerry, we remember, too, those unforgettable MGM productions, which stand out as landmarks in film history: *Singing in the Rain* and *The Bad and the Beautiful, North by Northwest* and *Scaramouche, Ivanhoe* and *The Prisoner of Zenda, The Picture of Dorian Gray* and *The Pirate*. We recall, as well, films made by Vincente Minnelli, Richard Brooks, George Sidney, Richard Thorpe, John Ford, Alfred Hitchcock, Anthony Mann, Nicholas Ray, and Joseph L. Mankiewicz.

As we discovered these masterpieces, we also discovered those amazing animated cartoons of William Hanna and Joseph Barbera, produced by Fred Quimby. Overshadowed by Walt Disney's artistic talent and commercial omnipotence, the impact of the Tom and Jerry series was underestimated in the United States.

The wealth of Tom and Jerry ranges from "Mouse in Manhattan" (1945), with its stunning line drawing, to the climax of "The Cat Concerto" (1947), rightly rewarded with an Oscar; from "Designs on Jerry" (1955), whose incredible trap is an idea of pure genius, to "Blue Cat Blues" (1956), which rehearses the great themes of melodrama. This vast saga deserves our attention, and its (re)discovery is now in order.

METRO-GOLDWYN-MAYER BEFORE TOM AND JERRY: HUGH HARMAN, RUDOLF ISING, AND FRED QUIMBY

Formed in 1924 by the merger of Loew's Incorporated with Goldwyn Pictures and Louis B. Mayer Productions, by the end of the 1920s Metro-Goldwyn-Mayer employed some of the most remarkable directors of the time: Victor Sjöström (alias Seastrom), King Vidor, Tod Browning, Rex Ingram, Clarence Brown, Erich von Stroheim. Its prestigious group of contract players included Lon Chaney and Greta Garbo, Norma Shearer and Marion Davies, Buster Keaton and Ramon Novarro, John Gilbert and Lionel Barrymore.

Within a few years, the company had an exceptional list of masterworks: *Greed, The Crowd, The Cameraman, The Big Parade, La Bohème, The Unholy Three, The Merry Widow, Flesh and the Devil, The Student Prince in Old Heidelberg, The Unknown, The Trail of '98, The Wind, He Who Gets Slapped.*

Although briefly supplanted by Warner Brothers, MGM weathered the transition to talking pictures triumphantly. The long-underdeveloped department of animated film emerged in

1934 with the Happy Harmonies series produced by Hugh Harman and Rudolf Ising.

Hugh Harman (1903–1982), the brother of Fred H. Harman, the creator of Red Ryder, met Rudolf Ising, also born in 1903, while they were both working for the Kansas City Film Agency.

Harman and Ising, together with Ub Iwerks and Walt Disney, shared in the venture into animation produced by Laugh-O-Gram Films. Both men left Disney—Ising in 1927 and Harman in 1928—to form Harman-Ising the following year. In 1930 they produced the first Looney Tunes for Leon Schlesinger, distributed by Warner Brothers. Then, in 1931, they created the Merrie Melodies series. In 1933, when budgetary problems arose with Schlesinger, Harman and Ising accepted an offer from Metro-Goldwyn-Mayer at twice their previous salaries.

They went to MGM and produced the Happy Harmonies series in the Silly Symphonies style that brought fame to Disney in 1928. Four years after their arrival they signed a production contract with Metro for the seven years to follow.

At the same time, MGM put Fred Quimby in charge of the company's animation department, which achieved brilliance with the arrival of the Tom and Jerry series.

Fred C. Quimby, born in Minneapolis in 1896, worked in journalism before taking over the management of a film theater in Missoula, Montana, in 1907. In 1913, he joined Pathé, where

he soon rose through the ranks to positions of important responsibility in their Salt Lake City and Denver offices. He became senior sales manager for Pathé and was put in charge of East Coast business. He became a member of its board of directors as well. Settling in New York, he stayed with Pathé until 1921, then went into production and distribution on his own. In 1924, he went to Fox and completely reorganized its short films department. In 1927, MGM made him head of sales and distribution for short films, and ten years later Fred Quimby became head of the department, especially supervising the production of animated films.

Wanting to hire a real cartoonist (Hugh Harman and Rudolf Ising were not yet under contract at that time), Fred Quimby called on Friz Freleng, one of Warner's veteran crew. He offered him the chance to supervise production and create a character that could compete with the winners from the other studios—Mickey, Bugs Bunny, Popeye, etc. "Quimby painted an idyllic picture, telling me I could hire anyone I wanted," said Freleng. He accepted and soon discovered that MGM had bought the rights to the comic strip "The Captain and the Kids." He thought this was a mistake. The series of cartoons drawn from it was actually a failure, and Freleng returned to work with Leon Schlesinger at Warner, thus leaving the field free for Hugh Harman, Rudolf Ising, and for those hired by Quimby: William Hanna, Bob Allen, Joseph Barbera, Jack Zander, Dan Gordon, Ray Kelly, Paul Sommer.

Under Fred Quimby's direction, Hugh Harman and Rudolf Ising contributed to the creation of quality cartoons whose importance should not be overlooked. Mark Meyerson wrote, "Harman and Ising had the only studio in the thirties that could compete with Disney in the beauty and opulence of their animation films. Each of these films, individually considered, displays a captivating animation technique, and fascinating decor and effects. Seen as a series they grow repetitive, but the beauty of these films is undeniable, and some of them remain real jewels." Mike Barrier has added, "Even their best films are incomplete, like flowers that have never fully bloomed."

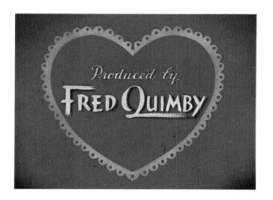

These reservations cannot diminish one's admiration of the quality and the care lavished on these productions, which include several really successful films. Just a few examples include "The Old Plantation" (1935), in which Simon Legree makes his appearance; "Bottles" (1936); "The Wayward Pups" (1937), in which a cat and two puppies confront a huge, nasty dog; "Pipe Dreams" (1938), with its orchestra of pipes and cigarette butts that sing and dance; "Art Gallery" (1939), a very curious film in which Nero sets fire to a picture representing Rome, with a cast of characters including Cleopatra, Beethoven, and Dr. Jekyll; "Peace on Earth" (1939), praised for its pacifism and nominated for an Oscar; "The Homeless Flea" (1940), with a red-nosed insect for a star.

These cartoons by Harman and Ising, although remarkably

accomplished, suffer from their length, which sometimes creates the impression of slow pacing. Above all, they lack the presence of regular heroes capable of developing into a series and into a real product of appeal to the viewer. At Warner Brothers, conversely, the cartoons were so popular that they were advertised in large type, like the big films. We should not forget that in 1937 Warner Brothers released thirty-six animated films made by directors such as Frank Tashlin, Fred "Tex" Avery, Friz Freleng, and Bob Clampett. One can see the sizable gap separating MGM from its competitor.

It was in 1940 that Metro produced "Puss Gets the Boot," the first of a series of 114 films that would enable the company to create two unforgettable characters: Tom, the cat and Jerry, the mouse.

William Hanna and Joseph Barbera: The Creators of "Tom and Jerry"

William Hanna and Joseph Barbera

Joseph Barbera

Joseph Barbera was born in New York in 1905 to Vincent and Frances Barbera of Palermo, Italy. Educated at New York University and the American Institute of Banking, he went on to work at the Irving Trust Company in New York, drawing during his free time and regularly receiving rejection slips from the various publications he submitted his work to. *Colliers* finally accepted a drawing and Barbera became a regular contributor to various magazines, ultimately leaving the world of finance. "Animation was something I really wanted to do," he confessed. He wrote to Walt Disney, who did not grant him an interview. "I'm glad he didn't," he remarked. "I would probably have become a devoted member of his team and would still be at the Disney Studios today." Barbera became a draftsman, and then an animator for Van Beuren Associates, a cartoon studio in the Bronx. In 1937 he was hired by MGM to work on Harman and Ising's productions.

William Hanna

William Hanna was born in 1911 in Melrose, New Mexico. He studied journalism at UCLA, became an engineer for a short time, but left his job to become a draftsman. In 1931 he was hired to work for Hugh Harman and Rudolph Ising on a temporary basis. In 1937, he became a full-time employee. He has defined his first tasks as follows: "To go for coffee, sweep up, wash the cells and drown the bosses in ideas." He eventually became director and story editor. He directed the second cartoon, "Blue Monday" (1938), of the Captain and the Kids series, but production was called off due to the lack of adequate public response.

William Hanna and Joseph Barbera Together

By April 1938, Hanna and Barbera were a team. Barbera declared, "We understood each other perfectly, and each of us had deep respect for the other's work." Hanna's views were similar: "I always wanted to be a director. So did Joe. Our only problem was finding the big chance."

This "big chance" was "Puss Gets the Boot"! For seventeen years, from 1940 to 1957, William Hanna and Joseph Barbera devoted themselves almost wholly to Tom and Jerry creating, under Fred Quimby's guidance, a series of fine cartoons, their excellence defined by the direction of Hanna and Barbera.

THE FIRST PERIOD:
1940–1957

114 FILMS

1940 This was the year of John Ford's *The Grapes of Wrath*, Hitchcock's *Rebecca*, Frank Borzage's *The Mortal Storm* and *Strange Cargo*, Ernst Lubitsch's *The Shop Around the Corner*, Chaplin's *The Great Dictator*, Ruben Mamoulian's *The Sign of Zorro*, and Michael Curtiz's *The Sea Hawk*. It was a magnificent year. Despite the rise of Nazism (as marked by both *The Great Dictator* and *The Mortal Storm*) and the consequent loss of part of the foreign market, Hollywood's cinema was resplendent. It was this same year that saw the emergence of the phenomenal Woody Woodpecker cartoon at Walter Lantz Productions and of Tom and Jerry at Metro-Goldwyn-Mayer.

"Puss Gets the Boot"

"PUSS GETS THE BOOT"

The origin of the wonderful Tom and Jerry series was a simple cartoon with only one name on its credits list: Rudolf Ising. Its two real creators, William Hanna and Joseph Barbera, remained in obscurity. The cat was not yet called Tom, but Jasper, and the mouse had no name. Following the suggestions of Fred Quimby, who was not yet satisfied by the single regular character of MGM's cartoons, the carefree Barney Bear, Hanna and Barbera had for a long time been trying to invent a real couple as heroes. "We wanted to find an opposition between two characters that could generate humor, and create basic situations, which we could develop into new stories and new adventures. We chose a dog and a fox before finally deciding upon a cat and a mouse." The names of Tom and Jerry given to the two characters had first been attached to a series produced by the Van Beuren studios in 1931–1933, but without a cat or mouse.

Fred Quimby, to whom Hanna and Barbera presented their project, was hardly delighted; he thought the idea was ridiculous. "What can you do that's original with a cat and a mouse?"

Hanna and Barbera took advantage of the situation, nonetheless, to get some other stories under way, hoping to present Fred Quimby with a completed project. The names of Tom and Jerry were finally chosen in a competition organized among the studio personnel.

"Puss Gets the Boot" was favorably received on its release, and the film was nominated for an Oscar. Metro-Goldwyn-Mayer was unaccustomed to having this kind of attention paid to its cartoons. William Hanna and Joseph Barbera had won the first battle.

"Puss Gets the Boot" marks the dividing line between two styles. It does, unquestionably, owe a great deal to the films already produced by Hugh Harman and Rudolf Ising. It has their technical quality, but also their tendency to slowness of pace. The cartoon is unusually long. The style of Hanna and Barbera is, on the other hand, evident in the way the two characters, Jasper (soon to be Tom) and the mouse, react to each other, and by the presence of Mammy Two Shoes, the unforgettable black maid, who will be seen in seventeen more episodes, until 1952.

While Tom and Jerry developed quite rapidly, changing even the way they looked, Mammy Two Shoes kept the same accent and drawl and, for most of the time, the same clothes (slippers, flower-printed bathrobe, stockings with reinforced or darned heels). She often called Tom "You no-good cat (in "Mouse Cleaning"), and exclaimed (in "Old Rockin' Chair Tom"): "Thomas, if you're a mouse catcher, then I'm Lana Turner, which I'm not!" Mammy Two Shoes made a wonderful foil for the devilish couple, appealing to Tom when Jerry frightened her or threatening to put Tom out if he continued to empty the refrigerator or sack the house.

The face of Mammy Two Shoes was deliberately hidden. We usually saw only the lower half of her body; the black maid's chin appeared once, as an exception, in "Part Time Pal," and the film's last shot showed Mammy Two Shoes far in the distance, pursuing Tom without our being able to see her features clearly.

Fred Quimby explained this in an article published in a 1951 edition of *The Hollywood Reporter*: "A young lady, after seeing a Tom and Jerry cartoon, inquired about the maid's face, which is never shown. To quote her (and we have it in writing lest there be any doubters among you): 'It gave me the impression that the operators in the booth must be having some sort of party, since every time the maid came on the screen, the only thing I could see was her feet. My curiosity is killing me. Before I go stark, raving mad, please tell me what she looks like.' In this instance, we had an artist draw a special head of the maid to accompany the reply. We also explained that since Tom and Jerry were the stars of the pictures, we did not wish to do anything that might distract attention from them."

THE BLACK MAID

(MAMMY TWO SHOES)

(1940) **Puss Gets the Boot**

(1941) **The Midnight Snack**

(1942) **Fraidy Cat**

(1942) **Dog Trouble**

(1942) **Puss 'n' Toots**

(1943) **The Lonesome Mouse**

(1945) **The Mouse Comes to Dinner**

(1947) **A Mouse in the House**

(1948) **Old Rockin' Chair Tom**

(1948) **Mouse Cleaning**

(1949) **Polka-Dot Puss**

(1949) **The Little Orphan**

(1950) **Saturday Evening Puss**

(1950) **The Framed Cat**

(1951) **Sleepy-Time Tom**

(1952) **Triplet Trouble**

(1952) **Push-Button Kitty**

IMMEDIATE PERFECTION

While Jerry had his definitive appearance from the very first cartoon, Tom underwent a number of changes. His ears, at first too big, grew smaller, and his features grew sharper, making the character more human, with a thinner, more thoroughbred face. "The Midnight Snack," the second film in the series, lists the names of William Hanna, Joseph Barbera, and Fred Quimby in its credits. This exceptional trio, to which we owe this saga's finest work, was already formed. Occasional traces of the gentleness inherited from Harman and Ising's productions would appear, as in "The Night Before Christmas," but on the whole, the series' major themes and lines of direction were set. The underlying cruelty and violence erupted at times (Tom slips on a cheese grater in "The Midnight Snack" before finding himself locked inside a refrigerator) and certain current expressions were visually literalized, so that Tom has a shiver up his spine while listening to the terrifying adventures of the radio series "The Witching Hour."

Tom and Jerry, suddenly reconciled in the face of a common enemy in "Dog Trouble" (1942), confront a mastiff appropriately named Bull Dog, as intolerant as he is aggressive. This very early incarnation of Spike, the recurring bulldog character, embodied brute force, while Spike evolved into a sympathetic character, regularly siding with Jerry against Tom.

William Hanna and Joseph Barbera divided their labor quite neatly. Hanna set up the storyboards, while Barbera was mainly in charge of stories and drawings. Hanna said of Barbera, "Joseph had, more than anyone I've ever met, the ability to capture appearance and expression in a quick sketch." Leonard Maltin, in *Of Mice and Magic,* defined the Hanna-Barbera production by characterizing Hanna's style as that of Harman and Ising, with its sweetness and human warmth. Barbera's strength lay in the gag. Hanna liked to direct and had a real sense of pace, while Barbera found creative fulfillment as a writer. They complemented each other perfectly.

Hanna noted, "Joe and I often disagreed, but we could always settle our differences of opinion. We discussed our projects. Joe then worked with the writers and the gagmen, and I with the animators."

The Tom and Jerry cartoons, shot in fairly grand style and with a team of first-rate draftsmen and animators, commanded a budget of $50,000 each, an exceptional sum. One should know, by way of comparison, that in 1942 *For Me and My Gal,* directed by Busby Berkeley with Judy Garland and Gene Kelly, cost $802,000 and that Vincente Minnelli's first film, *Cabin in the Sky,* made that same year, cost $662,000. Metro-Goldwyn-Mayer, now convinced of the importance and usefulness of its animation production, did its best to insure a quality that would match the perfection of all its other departments.

"The Lonesome Mouse" (1943)

THE ARRIVAL OF TEX AVERY

1942 While William Hanna and Joseph Barbera were busy making five animated cartoons for the Tom and Jerry series, two other films, "Blitz Wolf" and "The Early Bird Dood It," revealed the emergence of a new animator who wholly unsettled MGM.

Tex Avery, known while working at Warner as Fred Avery, found a position at MGM that allowed him to give free rein to

"Dr. Jekyll and Mr. Mouse" (1947)

"Puss 'n' Toots" (1942)

his wildest gags and his most outrageous puns. It was at Metro that Tex Avery, freer and more explosive than he had ever been at Warner, created Droopy and the mad squirrel, the libidinous wolf, George and Junior, as well as a gallery of sexy vamps. Michael Lah compared Tex's arrival to an avalanche, saying that "his way of working was quite mad," and it soon spread to Hanna and Barbera. An intense competition developed in which each film was faster than the preceding one, so that eventually only those who had worked on the film could understand it. In fact, after viewing a film one day, Quimby said that it went so fast that he couldn't remember it without seeing it again. He had to see it three times before he could understand it.

Fred Quimby's business acumen (according to Tex Avery, he knew nothing about scripts, gags, or anything else, and admitted it) lay in leaving Hanna, Barbera, and Avery entirely free rather than imposing his own ideas and thus running the risk of inhibiting their powers of invention. Avery's evident influence on the Tom and Jerry series was due not only to Avery's own presence at MGM, but also to the admiration existing between the two teams. Since they were using the same musician—the brilliant Scott Bradley—and, frequently, the same artists, from draftsman on down the line, the two teams inevitably exchanged ideas and emulated one another. One can imagine the various artists and technicians at lunch together in the studio canteen, proudly and zestfully exchanging their latest finds. The following examples represent only a few of the hundred inventions created by Hanna and Barbera but similar in style to Avery:

- the "wolf pacifier" hammer used by the white cat in "The Mouse Comes to Dinner" (1945) to calm energetic Tom

- the multiplication of Nibbles's eyes in "The Little Orphan" (1949)

- the woodpecker who pecks at Tom in "Hatch Up Your Troubles" (1949), so that the water, which the cat can't hold, leaks through the many holes

- Tom closing a door by sliding his paw around from the other side in "Jerry and the Lion" (1950)

- Jerry and Goldy, the fish, passing through Tom's head in "Jerry and the Goldfish" (1951)

- Tom breaking into pieces on contact with water in "Cat Napping" (1951)

- Tom digging his own grave and smoking a last cigarette before being crushed by the fall of an anvil in "The Duck Doctor" (1952)

"Two Little Indians" (1953)

1943: "THE YANKEE DOODLE MOUSE" A FIRST OSCAR FOR TOM AND JERRY!

The Tom and Jerry series, already twice nominated for the Oscar, was finally crowned with the long-awaited award. Six more followed. Metro-Goldwyn-Mayer's animation department had won out, and Hollywood's film industry rewarded the qual-

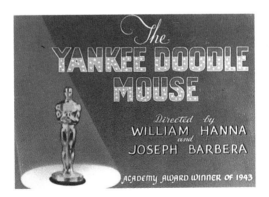

ity of a celebrated team. America and Japan were now at war in the Pacific, and "The Yankee Doodle Mouse" was a dazzling contribution to "the war effort," celebrating the courage of Lieutenant Jerry Mouse confronting a Tom who personified the Japanese enemy. In one of the film's finest gags, Tom and Jerry, threatened by a lighted stick of dynamite, try passing it to each other and, suddenly, caught in the heat of action, each one tries to take it back, instead. The victim of the final explosion is, as one might expect, Tom.

From 1944 on, Tom acquired his definitive look for the Hanna-Barbera period, which lasted until 1957. The head, face, and body were refined, and the animation perfected. Tex Avery's influence was evident when Tom, in "The Zoot Cat" (1944), began talking to his ladylove in the voice of Charles Boyer, or when, in "The Million Dollar Cat" (1944), his eyes suddenly popped out at the sight of Jerry, who was not supposed to be there.

TOM, JERRY, AND THE OSCARS

(1940) Puss Gets the Boot (nomination)

(1941) The Night Before Christmas (nomination)

(1943) The Yankee Doodle Mouse (Oscar)

(1944) Mouse Trouble (Oscar)

(1945) Quiet Please (Oscar)

(1946) The Cat Concerto (Oscar)

(1947) Dr. Jekyll and Mr. Mouse (nomination)

(1949) The Little Orphan (Oscar)

(1949) Hatch Up Your Troubles (nomination)

(1951) Jerry's Cousin (nomination)

(1952) The Two Mouseketeers (Oscar)

(1953) Johann Mouse (Oscar)

(1954) Touché, Pussy Cat! (nomination)

WAS JERRY A FEMALE?

Although Tom's sex is clearly defined as that of a male cat, Jerry's has a troubling ambiguity, created by a single shot in "Baby Puss" (1943). When Tom surprises Jerry in his bath, the mouse has a purely feminine reaction, which could support the notion that Jerry is a woman, although we do see him kissing the white kitten desired by his feline enemy ("Puss 'n' Toots," 1942; "Texas Tom," 1950; "Casanova Cat," 1951). In "Fine Feathered Friend" (1942), Jerry struts like a strip-tease artist, but in several other cartoons, Jerry has love problems with a female mouse. So, is the mouse male or female? The creators of

Tom and Jerry seem to have chosen not to close themselves in by any of the possible solutions, in order to fully exploit situations and their variations and to play on the couple and its ambivalence. Once Jerry is in the position to replace Tom for the attractive white kitten, anything goes—including Tom's frankly obscene gesture in "The Mouse Comes to Dinner" (1945), when he strikes a match on Jerry's behind. Nobody's perfect!

A SUCCESSION OF MASTERPIECES

"Solid Serenade" (1946)

Fred Quimby's view notwithstanding, the unending struggle between a cat and a mouse gave rise to a great variety of surprising situations. The talent of the series' creators, like a kaleidoscope whose basic elements produce wholly different compositions, created cartoons remarkable for both their originality and their formal beauty. In this respect, "Mouse in Manhattan" (1945) in which Jerry confronts New York alone (without Tom, who has stayed in the country), is a pure jewel. The splendor of the drawing lends real intensity to this parable in which the infinitesimally small (Jerry) comes up against the infinitely great (the city), finally concluding that there's no place like home.

"Tee for Two" (1945) is an amusing variation on the theme of golf, but the film also contains one of the most punishing scenes of the whole series, in which the unfortunate Tom, chased by a swarm of bees, tries to escape by hiding in water. Jerry treacherously points out Tom's position to the bees, and like bombers in formation, they swoop down upon their target and invade the reed through which Tom is breathing while under water. Maddened with pain, uttering an outrageous yelp, Tom empties the pond in one breath. The violence that tended to lend spice to Tom and Jerry's adventures rarely attained quite that level of cruelty!

In "Springtime for Thomas" (1946), Tom's love for a white kitten troubles Jerry, who sees it as the end of a long friendship, and he has to bring in a rival, a street cat named "Dream Boy." In "Solid Serenade" (1946), Tom sings to his ladylove:

> I gotta gal who's always late
> Every time we have a date
> But I love her
> I'm gonna ask her
> Is you is or . . . is you ain't my baby?

Tom's amorous passion doesn't prevent his falling victim to Jerry, who has found an ally in "Killer" the dog, a vindictive version of Spike.

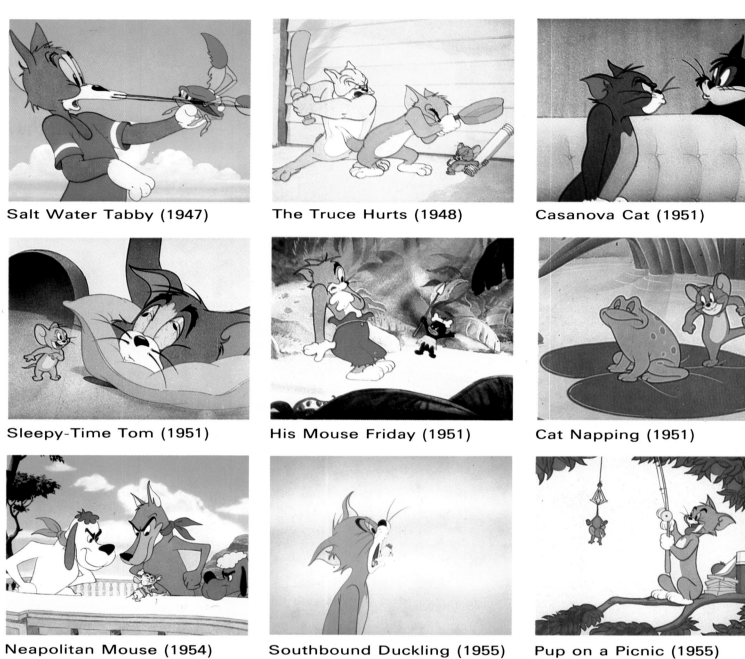

Salt Water Tabby (1947)

The Truce Hurts (1948)

Casanova Cat (1951)

Sleepy-Time Tom (1951)

His Mouse Friday (1951)

Cat Napping (1951)

Neapolitan Mouse (1954)

Southbound Duckling (1955)

Pup on a Picnic (1955)

The Yankee Doodle Mouse (1943)

Solid Serenade (1946)

Texas Tom (1950)

The Framed Cat (1950)

Touché, Pussy Cat! (1954)

Smarty Cat (1955)

THE FIRST PERIOD

William Hanna and Joseph Barbera (1940—1957)

Title	production number	copyright number	copyright year	release date
PUSS GETS THE BOOT	42	5742	40	02-20-40
THE MIDNIGHT SNACK	60	6999	41	07-19-41
THE NIGHT BEFORE CHRISTMAS	78	7739	41	12-06-41
FRAIDY CAT	69	7415	42	01-17-42
DOG TROUBLE	64	7833	42	04-18-42
PUSS 'N' TOOTS	74	8113	42	05-30-42
THE BOWLING ALLEY-CAT	79	8137	42	07-18-42
FINE FEATHERED FRIEND	81	8405	42	10-10-42
SUFFERIN' CATS!	85	8607	42	01-16-43
THE LONESOME MOUSE	89	8869	43	05-22-43
THE YANKEE DOODLE MOUSE	91	8895	43	06-26-43
BABY PUSS	99	8885	43	12-25-43
THE ZOOT CAT	104	8989	44	02-26-44
THE MILLION DOLLAR CAT	109	9112	44	05-06-44
THE BODYGUARD	114	9269	44	07-22-44
PUTTIN' ON THE DOG	117	9368	44	10-28-44
MOUSE TROUBLE	118	9557	44	11-23-44
THE MOUSE COMES TO DINNER	123	9698	45	05-05-45
MOUSE IN MANHATTAN	132	10782	45	07-07-45
TEE FOR TWO	126	9867	45	07-21-45
FLIRTY BIRDY	129	9919	45	09-22-45
QUIET PLEASE	131	11020	45	12-22-45
SPRINGTIME FOR THOMAS	137	10181	46	03-30-46
THE MILKY WAIF	142	11359	46	05-18-46
TRAP HAPPY	145	11482	46	06-29-46
SOLID SERENADE	149	11553	46	03-31-46
CAT FISHIN'	155	11773	46	02-22-47
PART TIME PAL	153	11727	46	03-15-47
THE CAT CONCERTO	165	11976	46	04-26-47
DR. JEKYLL AND MR. MOUSE	157	11854	46	06-14-47
SALT WATER TABBY	158	12030	47	07-12-47
A MOUSE IN THE HOUSE	162	12120	47	08-30-47
THE INVISIBLE MOUSE	163	12227	47	09-27-47
KITTY FOILED	167	12366	47	06-01-48
THE TRUCE HURTS	173	12503	47	07-17-48
OLD ROCKIN' CHAIR TOM	172	12602	47	09-18-48
PROFESSOR TOM	179	12772	48	10-30-48
MOUSE CLEANING	182	12876	48	12-11-48
POLKA-DOT PUSS	184	12914	48	02-26-49
THE LITTLE ORPHAN	191	13132	48	04-30-49
HATCH UP YOUR TROUBLES	186	13012	48	05-14-49
HEAVENLY PUSS	189	13062	48	07-09-49
THE CAT AND THE MERMOUSE	194	13268	49	09-03-49
LOVE THAT PUP	197	13390	49	10-01-49
JERRY'S DIARY [ ]	198	13427	49	10-22-49
TENNIS CHUMPS	200	13445	49	12-10-49
LITTLE QUACKER	209	13793	50	01-07-50
SATURDAY EVENING PUSS	206	13634	50	01-14-50
TEXAS TOM	210	13718	50	03-11-50
JERRY AND THE LION	201	13532	50	04-08-50
SAFETY SECOND	212	13844	50	07-01-50
TOM AND JERRY IN THE HOLLYWOOD BOWL	224	14219	50	09-16-50

	production number	copyright number	copyright year	release date		production number	copyright number	copyright year	release date
THE FRAMED CAT	214	13939	50	10-21-50	BABY BUTCH	277	16415	53	03-14-54
CUEBALL CAT	215	14094	50	11-25-50	MICE FOLLIES	279	16494	53	09-04-54
CASANOVA CAT	216	14173	50	01-06-51	NEAPOLITAN MOUSE	281	16604	53	10-02-54
JERRY AND THE GOLDFISH	219	14235	51	03-03-51	DOWNHEARTED DUCKLING	283	16691	53	11-13-54
JERRY'S COUSIN	220	14427	51	04-07-51	PET PEEVE	296	17021	54	11-20-54
SLEEPY-TIME TOM	223	14486	51	05-26-51	TOUCHÉ, PUSSY CAT!	294	16903	54	12-18-54
HIS MOUSE FRIDAY	227	14580	51	07-07-51	SOUTHBOUND DUCKLING	298	17065	54	03-12-55
SLICKED-UP PUP	233	14829	51	09-08-51	PUP ON A PICNIC	285	16739	53	04-30-55
NIT-WITTY KITTY	231	14680	51	10-06-51	MOUSE FOR SALE	287	16740	53	05-21-55
CAT NAPPING	229	14645	51	12-08-51	DESIGNS ON JERRY	292	16845	53	09-02-55
THE FLYING CAT	233	14841	51	01-12-52	TOM AND CHERIE	299	17445	55	09-09-55
THE DUCK DOCTOR	235	14936	52	02-16-52	SMARTY CAT	299	17064	54	10-14-55
THE TWO MOUSEKETEERS	247	15281	52	03-15-52	PECOS PEST	289	16815	53	11-11-55
SMITTEN KITTEN [ ]	240	14985	52	04-12-52	THAT'S MY MOMMY	300	17667	55	11-19-55
TRIPLET TROUBLE	238	15051	52	04-19-52	THE FLYING SORCERESS	301	17689	55	01-27-56
LITTLE RUNAWAY	242	15101	52	06-14-52	THE EGG AND JERRY	314	13012	56	03-23-56
FIT TO BE TIED	243	15202	52	07-26-52	BUSY BUDDIES	303	17832	56	05-04-56
PUSH-BUTTON KITTY	244	15251	52	09-06-52	MUSCLE BEACH TOM	304	17858	56	—
CRUISE CAT [ ]	252	15420	51	10-18-52	DOWNBEAT BEAR	305	17936	56	—
THE DOG HOUSE	250	15371	52	11-29-52	BLUE CAT BLUES	306	17981	56	—
THE MISSING MOUSE	254	15545	52	01-10-53	BARBECUE BRAWL	307	18093	56	—
JERRY AND JUMBO	256	15640	51	02-21-53	TOPS WITH POPS	318	13390	56	—
JOHANN MOUSE	266	16167	52	03-21-53	TIMID TABBY	308	18196	56	—
THAT'S MY PUP	260	15812	52	04-25-53	FEEDIN' THE KIDDIE	321	13132	56	—
JUST DUCKY	258	15694	51	09-05-53	MUCHO MOUSE	310	18289	56	—
TWO LITTLE INDIANS	262	15858	52	10-17-53	TOM'S PHOTO FINISH	311	18308	56	—
LIFE WITH TOM [ ]	264	15947	52	11-21-53	HAPPY GO DUCKY	309	18266	56	—
PUPPY TALE	275	16312	53	01-23-54	ROYAL CAT NAP	317	18430	57	—
POSSE CAT	268	15996	52	01-30-54	THE VANISHING DUCK	325	18515	57	—
HIC-CUP PUP	270	16098	52	04-17-54	ROBIN HOODWINKED	329	18582	57	—
LITTLE SCHOOL MOUSE	273	16112	52	05-29-54	TOT WATCHERS	330	18649	57	—

The sign [ ] indicates that the cartoon includes one or several extracts (reused) of other, preceding cartoons.
Note that the order of production does not necessarily correspond to that of films' release.

Little Quacker (1950)

Tennis Chumps (1949)

Two Little Indians(1953)

Hic-Cup Pup (1954)

Designs on Jerry (1955)

Designs on Jerry (1955)

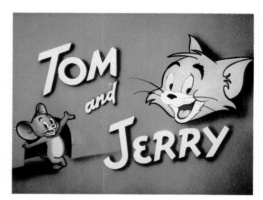

Mouse Cleaning (1948)

Mouse Cleaning (1948)

Hatch up your Troubles (1949)

The Flying Cat (1952)

Jerry and Jumbo (1953)

Two Little Indians (1953)

Pup on a Picnic (1955)

Mouse for Sale (1955)

Designs on Jerry (1955)

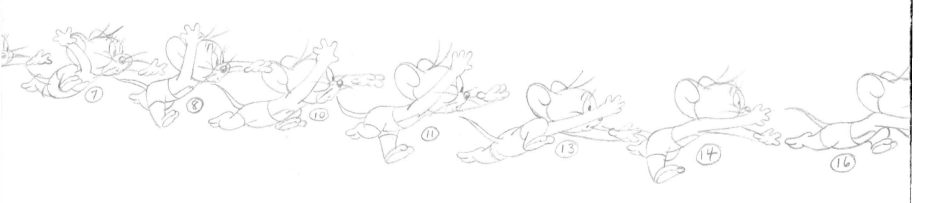

NEXT STOP HOLLYWOOD:
JERRY DANCES WITH GENE KELLY!

Anchors Aweigh, whose cast included Frank Sinatra, Kathryn Grayson, Jose Iturbi, Gene Kelly, Dean Stockwell, and Rags Ragland, was produced by Joe Pasternak. George Sidney was assigned to direct this musical comedy, which narrates the many adventures of two sailors on furlough in Hollywood. The script had alternating musical and romantic sequences, but Gene Kelly wanted something really new and original in the film. "For several days," said Kelly, "Stanley Donen and I watched the search for 'this something,' and then, after a long silence, Stanley suggested, 'Why don't we have a dance with a cartoon?'" The project was proposed to Louis B. Mayer, who hesitated, unable to visualize it. Joe Pasternak took the matter up with Mayer and with Eddie Mannix, a studio executive. Mannix advised Gene Kelly and Stanley Donen to call Walt Disney for advice. Disney, who was at that time involved with a similar experiment in *The Three Caballeros,* was enthusiastic and acknowledged that Kelly's plan for the sequence was clearly further advanced than his own efforts. "I'll always be grateful to Walt," said Kelly, because he telephoned Eddie Mannix to tell him what a fine idea we had, and to assure him of the feasibility of such a sequence." That was all Mannix and Mayer wanted to hear. They allowed Pasternak to shoot the scene.

In spite of Kelly's and Donen's request, however, Disney would not direct this sequence in his own studios. It was MGM's animation department who got the assignment. William Hanna and Joseph Barbera worked under the direction of Fred Quimby, whose assistant, Irving G. Ries, supervised the optical effects department. The scene took two months to produce; it cost $100,000 and delayed the film's release. The result, which surpassed everyone's expectations, still remains, forty years after its production, a dazzling display of technical perfection and humor.

The scene shows Gene Kelly in a sailor's costume—cap, striped T-shirt, and white pants—entering a strange land inhabited by Disney-like birds and animals. He learns the king has imposed a dreadful law that forbids music. The sailor goes to the castle, where he encounters the king (Jerry) seated on his throne, while his faithful servant (also Jerry) vainly offers him cheese. "I'm alone," Jerry complains. The sailor reproaches him for his behavior. "I can't sing or dance," says Jerry, "so I've imposed a law against it." "Anyone can, you just have to want to," responds the sailor, who then undertakes to show Jerry how. Jerry begins to learn. He does a tap dance with Kelly. Other sailors join in. They jump over each other, and Jerry

passes from one sailor's shoulders to the next. Jerry, now wonderstruck, gives the sailor a medal in recognition of his newfound dancing ability. "And that's how I got my medal," explains Gene Kelly to the children listening to his story. The sequence is composed of three musical numbers: "Melancholy Mouse" (Jackson), "I Hadda" (Jackson), and "The Worry Song," composed by Ralph Freed and Sammy Fain. Kelly has stated that although he has received credit for the sequences, he could not have done them without Stanley Donen's help. Donen, working with the cameraman, set all the movement. Kelly said that it was not easy for the cameraman, who was being asked to film something that wasn't there. Kelly had first been filmed on a blue background, with Jerry then animated by rotoscope. The two images were later fused optically in a single shot.

One error stands to be corrected: Certain photographs show Tom, Jerry, and Gene Kelly in the same shot. These are actually photographic collages done for publicity and not real film shots. We never see Tom and Gene Kelly together. First, only Tom and Jerry, and later, Gene Kelly and Jerry. The success of this exceptional experiment encouraged MGM to relaunch a similar one seven years later in *Dangerous When Wet* by Charles Walters.

Gene Kelly and Jerry: *Anchors Aweigh* **(1945)**

"THE MILKY WAIF," OR THE ARRIVAL OF NIBBLES

Only six years after its first cartoon, the Tom and Jerry series was enhanced by a new character, a little mouse called Nibbles. He was different from Jerry with his gray color and boundless appetite. Cast as an orphan in "The Little Orphan" (1949), a king's musketeer in "The Two Mouseketeers" (1952), and accompanied by an alter ego in "Two Little Indians" (1953), Nibbles, with no change in physical appearance, was to take the name of Tuffy, beginning with "Little School Mouse" (1954). He turns up as apprentice musketeer in "Touché, Pussy Cat!" (1954), as full musketeer in "Tom and Cherie" (1955), and "Royal Cat Nap" (1958), and as Robin Hood's faithful companion in "Robin Hoodwinked" (1958). Unlike the more deliberate

"The Milky Waif" (1946)

Jerry, Tuffy embodied youthful impetuosity and daring, always ready to provoke Tom, to set off dangerous fireworks. Only in "Little School Mouse" (1954) does he stand for peaceful coexistence, finally urging Tom and Jerry, as his students, to be good friends.

APOTHEOSIS ("THE CAT CONCERTO") AND INCREASINGLY WICKED BEHAVIOR

The Cat Concerto," deservingly crowned with 1946's Oscar for the best animation film of the year, is one of the finest of the series. Tom's appearance as a virtuoso pianist, the struggle with Jerry all through Liszt's Hungarian Rhapsody no. 2, and the combination of music and animation remain unforgettable. Soon after, the series' tone started to take on a great deal of slapstick violence. The carefree Mammy Two Shoes is attacked by Tom in "Part Time Pal" (1947), suddenly a victim of the moody feline. In "Salt Water Tabby" (1947), Tom forsakes his usual gallantry and behaves like a real hooligan toward his ladylove by devouring her hot dog and shamelessly spitting water at her. A few weeks later, in "A Mouse in the House" (1947), Mammy Two Shoes is again the object of fun of both Tom and his rival.

The reversal of alliances began to fill the scripts of the various cartoons. Tom, Jerry, and Butch (Spike) sign a temporary non-aggression pact in "The Truce Hurts" (1948), and in "Professor Tom" (1948) Jerry ends up allying himself with a sympathetic nonviolent kitten against Tom!

The series had attained a matchless perfection, as in "Mouse Cleaning" (1948), which characterizes Tom's adventures in a dirty house he's perpetually forced to clean. The arrival of a coal truck transforms his adventure into a real nightmare.

"The Cat Concerto" (1947)

NIBBLES—TUFFY

(1946) **The Milky Waif**
(1949) **The Little Orphan**
(1950) **Safety Second**
(1952) **The Two Mouseketeers**
(1953) **Two Little Indians**
(1953) **Life with Tom** [1]
(1954) **Little School Mouse**
(1954) **Mice Follies**
(1954) **Touché, Pussy Cat!**
(1955) **Tom and Cherie**
(1957) **Feedin' the Kiddie** [2]
(1958) **Royal Cat Nap**
(1958) **Robin Hoodwinked**

1. Reuse of "The Little Orphan."
2. CinemaScope version of "The Little Orphan."

NEW RELEASES, REUSES, AND NEW CHARACTERS

In 1949, the Tom and Jerry series celebrated its tenth anniversary. Its variety and constantly renewed inspiration were at their height that year. Butch the dog and his son Pup—who a few years later became Spike and Tyke—made their appearance in "Love That Pup," whose musical theme became one of the most regularly used of the series. At the same time, MGM decided to make full use of the property represented by the series by rereleasing certain cartoons. Among them were "The Midnight Snack" (1941), rereleased on February 27, 1948; "Fine Feathered Friend" (1942), rereleased on January 1, 1949; "Sufferin' Cats" (1943), rereleased on June 4, 1949; "The Lonesome Mouse" (1943), rereleased on November 26, 1949. The fact that the cartoons with the "old" Tom and those with the definitive, slender, and sharper Tom were distributed simultaneously was not a prohibitive factor. In a similar fashion, William Hanna, Joseph Barbera, and Fred Quimby initiated the new technique of reuse with "Jerry's Diary" (1949). The system was simple: Tom finds Jerry's personal diary and reads it, allowing the insertion of extracts from four preceding animation films: "Tee for Two" (1945), "Mouse Trouble" (1944), "Solid Serenade" (1946) and "The Yankee Doodle Mouse" (1943). The dexterity with which this "economical" system was put into effect was such that the film did not suffer from the presence of these already familiar images; but rather, they gained variety. This technique, highly perfected, was used on various occasions, with the reuse justified by the script. "Smitten Kitten" (1952) retraces the misadventures of Tom, Jerry's perpetual victim, and "Smarty Cat" (1955) recalls some of Tom's quarrels with Spike. In 1950, the duckling who became one of the series' regular heroes made his appearance. "Little Quacker" made the duckling both a new friend for Jerry and someone for Jerry to watch, somewhat like Nibbles, in the face of the danger.

THE DUCKLING

(1950) **Little Quacker**
(1952) **The Duck Doctor**
(1953) **Just Ducky**
(1954) **Downhearted Duckling**
(1955) **Southbound Duckling**
(1955) **That's My Mommy**
(1958) **Happy Go Ducky**
(1958) **The Vanishing Duck**

"The Duck Doctor" (1952)

"JERRY'S COUSIN" IS BEATEN BY GERALD McBOING BOING, AND MAMMY TWO SHOES CHANGES COLOR

"Jerry's Cousin" (1951)

Jerry's Cousin" (1951), nominated as the year's best animated cartoon, lost to Robert Cannon's "Gerald McBoing Boing." This event would not have mattered very much had it not also brought recognition of UPA (United Productions of America), whose animation techniques were to play a part in the transformation of the whole cartoon genre. Scenes, characters, and faces had been simplified for a more stylized look, and the animation was clearly less fluid than that of the great cartoons of the 1940s. This new, far less expensive style rapidly influenced the larger studios who, during this period of crisis induced by the arrival of television, were finding their animation departments far too costly.

The United States was increasingly torn by racial problems and—in 1954—the Supreme Court declared racial segregation unconstitutional. Hollywood had long been denouncing racism and antisemitism, and the Mammy Two Shoes character now became embarrassing. In order to reuse the cartoons in which she appeared, MGM decided to make the black maid, dear to the first Tom and Jerry films, into an Irish maid, whose drawl was replaced by a new voice. The cartoons were then freshly dubbed by June Foray, and the arms and black legs of Mammy Two Shoes were changed to white. Finally, after twelve years of faithful service, the character of Mammy Two Shoes was discontinued in "Push-Button Kitty" (1952).

TOM AND JERRY SWIM WITH ESTHER WILLIAMS

Dangerous When Wet (1953), directed by Charles Walters, had a cast composed of Esther Williams, Fernando Lamas, Jack Carson, Charlotte Greenwood, Denise Darcel, and William Demarest. The film follows the training and performance of Katy Higgins (Esther Williams), who succeeds in swimming across the English Channel. It includes a dream sequence in which we see Esther Williams, Tom, and Jerry swimming together. Sea horses, a giant octopus, a turtle, and a swordfish make their appearances. The octopus makes advances to Esther

Tom, Jerry, and Esther Williams: *Dangerous When Wet* (1953)

Williams who, drawn in opposite directions by him and by Tom and Jerry, finally wakes up. It was only a dream. The sequence, produced by Fred Quimby and directed by William Hanna and Joseph Barbera, appeared twenty-three years later in the compilation film *That's Entertainment, Part II.* Tom and Jerry went from short to feature film for the second time, and this scene, too, contributed to their fame.

But behind that fame lay another, less euphoric reality. The series' style was being undermined by both the influence of UPA and the rise in production costs. Its animation became increasingly schematic, due mostly to a decrease in the number of cells. The animation was no longer as rich, as is clearly shown in "Neapolitan Mouse" (1954) or "Downbeat Bear" (1956). The characters became schematic as well (the bear in "Downbeat Bear," the couple in "Pet Peeve," 1954). Mammy Two Shoes disappeared and was suddenly replaced by a young woman and her executive husband. This mistress appears either blond ("Mouse for Sale," 1955) or brunette ("The Flying Sorceress," 1956), with no explanation for the switch.

1955: The Departure of Fred Quimby

"Pecos Pest" (1955), the ninety-sixth cartoon of the Tom and Jerry series, was also the last whose credits listed the name of Fred Quimby. Hugh Harman left MGM in 1941 to start his own company. The next year, Rudolf Ising also left to shoot training films at the Hal Roach studio, nicknamed "Fort Roach." Fred Quimby remained alone at the head of the animation department until his own departure in 1955. He died ten years later on September 15, 1965.

William Hanna and Joseph Barbera, having lost their producer, directed "That's My Mommy" (1955) on their own. The popularity of CinemaScope, meant to prove the superiority of the film screen over television, forced them to make all their next films, from "The Egg and Jerry" (1956) to "Tot Watchers" (1958), in scope. The sixteen films shot in CinemaScope divide into thirteen new films and three remakes.

"The Egg and Jerry" (1956), "Tops with Pops" (1957), and "Feedin' the Kiddie" (1957) are actually only new CinemaScope versions of "Hatch Up Your Troubles" (1949), "Love That Pup" (1949), and "The Little Orphan" (1949). The animation of the versions is identical, but the colors have become more intense and the design has been reduced to a minimum. The care and quality that had prevailed in the first films gave way to results that were far less lavish. The original quality slackened, but the films were in CinemaScope and the distributors who had invested heavily in new equipment had cartoons in the new, fashionable format.

Hollywood was fighting for survival. The animated cartoon took part in the battle against television. The skill of William Hanna, Joseph Barbera, and their team allowed them to put off the day of reckoning. Some of the cartoons even had a very surprising tone. "Blue Cat Blues" (1956), one of the most curious of the series, has an unusually dark theme. Tom, ruined and betrayed by his beloved, gets drunk and tries to commit suicide. Jerry, his old enemy, consoles him until discovering that he too has been the victim of a faithless vamp. Reunited in suffering, the two former enemies prepare to commit double suicide.

Economy and sacrifice did not, however, save the animation department, and Joseph Barbera himself has related the end of this prestigious production: "We got a telephone call asking us to stop everything in production and to dismiss the whole animation unit. Twenty years of work were suddenly stopped by a mere phone call."

Fred Quimby

WILLIAM HANNA AND JOSEPH BARBERA LEAVE MGM

William Hanna

Three years after Tex Avery's departure in 1954, William Hanna and Joseph Barbera left Metro-Goldwyn-Mayer. While working on the Tom and Jerry series, they also made "Good Will to Men" (1956), a CinemaScope remake of "Peace on Earth," and two cartoons with Spike and Tyke, "Give and Tyke" (1957) and "Scat Cats" (1957). Louis B. Mayer was no longer there, and in 1957 Dore Schary also left.

Hanna and Barbera turned to television, then in full swing. On July 7, 1957, together with George Sidney, they formed Hanna-Barbera Productions Inc., with their own Hollywood studio at 3400 Cahuenga Boulevard. Joseph Barbera was president and William Hanna was vice-president. Their first production, "Ruff and Reddy," the story of a cat and dog, imposed new shooting standards and a budget that was much reduced in comparison to those at MGM: $2,800 instead of $50,000 for each short film. Today, Hanna and Barbera head a veritable

The Flintstones

empire of eight hundred employees. Their animated films are distributed in more than eighty countries. Outstanding among their sizable production are: "Ruff and Reddy" (1957–1960), "Huckleberry Hound" (1958–1962), "Augie Doggie and Doggie Daddy" (1959–1962), whose adventures recall those of Spike and Tyke, "Quick Draw McGraw" (1959–1962), "Yakky Doodle" (1960–1962), a little duck resembling the duckling protected from Tom's appetite by Jerry, "Yogi Bear" (1960–1962), "The Flintstones" (1960–1966), "Wally Gator" (1962), "The Jetsons" (1962–1963; 1985–1986), "Sinbad Jr." (1965), "Scooby-Doo" (1969–1974; 1976–1979), "Shazzan" (1967–1968), "Kwicky Koala" (1981–1982), "Smurfs" (1981–1987), "Challenge of the Gobots" (1984–1986).

In 1967, William Hanna and Joseph Barbera sold their studio (while retaining its directorship) to Taft Broadcasting and became part of Taft Entertainment Company. Barbera is president of the Greek and Huntington Hartford theaters, and chairman of the executive board of the Los Angeles City and County Earthquake Preparedness Committee. Hanna has a strong interest in navigation. Both men are involved with numerous charitable organizations.

Huckleberry Hound

Joseph Barbera

THE SECOND PERIOD

Gene Deitch (1960—1962)

	production number	copyright year
SWITCHIN' KITTEN	400	60
DOWN AND OUTING	401	61
IT'S GREEK TO ME-OW	402	61
HIGH STEAKS	404	61
MOUSE INTO SPACE	403	61
LANDING STRIPLING	406	61
CALYPSO CAT	407	61
DICKY MOE	408	61
TOM AND JERRY CARTOON KIT	405	61
TALL IN THE TRAP	410	62
SORRY SAFARI	409	62
BUDDIES THICKER THAN WATER	411	62
CARMEN GET IT!	412	62

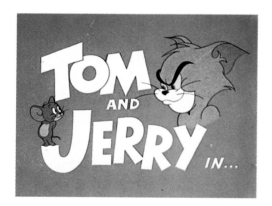

THE RETURN OF TOM AND JERRY

After the elimination of its animation department, MGM limited itself to periodic distribution of its old Tom and Jerry cartoons. In 1959, William L. Snyder signed a production contract with the company. Thirteen new cartoons with Tom and Jerry were to be directed by Gene Deitch.

Who was Gene Deitch? In 1955, Paul Terry had sold his studios to CBS, and the young Gene Deitch, then thirty-one years old, was assigned Terrytoon's new production. Deitch had worked for UPA and it was his stimulus that had led to the making of Ernest Pintoff's "Flebus" and Al Kouzel's "Gaston the Crayon."

In 1960 Deitch left for Prague, and it was there that thirteen new Tom and Jerry's were produced. He has stated that Metro was not interested in reviving Tom and Jerry, but only in drawing maximum profit from their popularity, with minimum investment. Their artists were solely responsible for the films' quality. Rumor has it that Deitch's coworkers had only six of the series' cartoons to use as models. The result, artistically speaking, could have been foreseen. The lively humor and creativity faded. Even though Tom and Jerry looked almost the same as before, these thirteen cartoons pale in comparison with the preceding ones. The carelessness of the music and sound effects only intensified the difference.

The house that served as the setting for Tom and Jerry's adventures, the animals around them, and the charged atmosphere now served as background for anonymous stories that could have been interpreted by any two characters. The plot lines almost never used the already established relationship between Tom the cat and Jerry the mouse.

You might notice that Tom's master bears a curious resemblance to Clinton Clobber, a Terrytoon character during Gene Deitch's period there. This is noticeable in "Down and Outing" (1961) and "High Steaks" (1962).

The mediocrity of these new cartoons clearly emphasized the quality of the preceding ones. MGM took advantage of this to combine some of those in "The Tom and Jerry Festival of Fun."

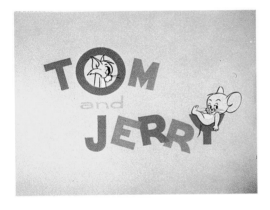

THE THIRD PERIOD

....

Chuck Jones, Jim Pabian, Abe Levitow, Tom Ray, Ben Washam (1963—1967)

		production number	copyright number	copyright year	director
PENTHOUSE MOUSE		500	20646	63	CJ
THE CAT ABOVE AND THE MOUSE BELOW		503	—	64	CJ
IS THERE A DOCTOR IN THE MOUSE?		506	—	64	CJ
MUCH ADO ABOUT MOUSING		501	—	64	CJ
SNOWBODY LOVES ME		502	20648	64	CJ
THE UNSHRINKABLE JERRY MOUSE		504	—	64	CJ
AH, SWEET MOUSE-STORY OF LIFE		507	20875	65	CJ
TOM-IC ENERGY		505	—	64	CJ
BAD DAY AT CAT ROCK		514	20971	65	CJ
THE BROTHERS CARRY-MOUSE-OFF		524	20763	66	JP
HAUNTED MOUSE		508	20906	65	CJ
I'M JUST WILD ABOUT JERRY		510	—	65	CJ
OF FELINE BONDAGE		509	20907	65	CJ
THE YEAR OF THE MOUSE		512	20944	65	CJ
THE CAT'S-ME OUCH		515	20987	65	CJ
JERRY-GO-ROUND		513	21022	65	AL
DUEL PERSONALITY		526	20817	67	CJ
JERRY, JERRY QUITE CONTRARY		535	20839	66	CJ
LOVE ME, LOVE MY MOUSE		519	20970	66	CJ
PUSS 'N' BOATS		518	21151	66	AL
FILET MEOW		525	21153	67	AL
MATINEE MOUSE	[ ]	534	21251	66	TR
THE A-TOM-INABLE SNOWMAN		532	21210	67	AL
CATTY CORNERED		521	21148	66	AL
CAT AND DUPLI-CAT		520	20762	67	CJ
O-SOLAR MEOW		517	21150	66	AL
GUIDED MOUSE-ILLE		516	21149	66	AL
ROCK 'N' RODENT		522	21152	67	AL
CANNERY RODENT		528	20840	67	CJ
THE MOUSE FROM H.U.N.G.E.R		531	21213	67	AL
SURF-BORED CAT		530	20904	67	AL
SHUTTER BUGGED CAT	[ ]	533	21497	67	TR
ADVANCE AND BE MECHANIZED		529	21235	67	BW
PURR-CHANCE TO DREAM		—	21270	67	BW

The sign [ ] indicates that the cartoon includes one or several extracts (reused) of other, preceding cartoons.

CHUCK JONES: FROM BUGS BUNNY TO TOM AND JERRY

The unfortunate experience of Gene Deitch's thirteen films proved to MGM that the Tom and Jerry label still held a considerable attraction for the public, and that nothing of any quality could be done without an adequate budget for these films. Metro called upon the services of Chuck Jones, a veteran of the Hollywood cartoon.

MGM gave Chuck Jones a relatively high budget— $42,000 for each cartoon—so that he would not find himself in Gene Deitch's situation, and by 1966 they took over SIB-Tower 12 Productions, thereby forming the MGM Animation-Visual Arts Department, with Chuck Jones at its head. Chuck Jones produced thirty-four new Tom and Jerry films. Eighteen were directed by Jones, one by Jim Pabian, ten by Abe Levitow, two by Tom Ray, two by Ben Washam, and one by Chuck Jones and Ben Washam together.

Unfortunately, the Hollywood cartoon was no longer what it had been, and what might have been a fascinating experience ended in a succession of films of very uneven quality. Chuck Jones was the first to admit this, saying that the characters were not his own, that he never understood them as well as he did the Road Runner and the Coyote. He felt that his Tom and Jerry were like the Road Runner and the Coyote disguised as cat and mouse! A new credits list was created, with Tom meowing inside the famous "Ars Gratia Arts" logo. He then curved into the O of "Tom," while Jerry posed nonchalantly in the arms of the Y in "Jerry."

Gene Deitch had contented himself with reproducing Tom and Jerry's usual appearance. Chuck Jones, however, sought to change it. Jerry now had larger ears, and Tom was given pointed ears and very heavy eyebrows, like Bela Lugosi, some said.

Chuck Jones and his coworkers did adapt certain ideas dear to the history of the cartoon. In "Tom-Ic Energy" (1965), Tom chases Jerry right into the sky and then, finding himself in the void, suddenly realizes the danger and falls. Similarly, in "Ah, Sweet Mouse-Story of Life" (1965), Tom and Jerry fall into the void. Jerry hooks onto a question mark, which slows his fall like a parachute. Tom hooks onto an exclamation mark and quickens his dizzying descent.

Like Gene Deitch, Chuck Jones appeared uninterested in recreating the atmosphere of the house that had formed a wonderful closed world in the series' first episodes. The action was scattered over various settings. Compared to the Hanna and Barbera cartoons of the 1940s, those done by Chuck Jones, who oversaw all the films, including those occasionally attributed to others, appear more stylized. The settings are similar, but the animation is smoother and more rapid than that of Gene Deitch's work.

Chuck Jones

Born September 21, 1912, in Spokane, Washington, Charles Martin Jones studied at the Chouinard Art Institute in Los Angeles before going to work with Ub Iwerks. He was hired by Leon Schlesinger, for whom he worked successively as draftsman, script writer, assistant, and director. By 1933 he was at Warner Brothers, where his colleagues were Friz Freleng, Fred "Tex" Avery, and Bob Clampett. Chuck Jones directed Daffy Duck, Bugs Bunny, and Elmer Fudd. This was the period of the cartoon's golden age at Warner Brothers. After a brief time spent as gagman for Walter Lantz, he returned to Warner, where he remained until 1963, when the company's animation department was closed. That same year, he founded SIB-Tower 12 Productions with Les Goldman, and became associated with MGM for the production of a Tom and Jerry series.

Jones had in addition gathered together some of his old companions from Warner Brothers: Ben Washam, Abe Levitow, Philip Deguard, Dick Thompson, and Tom Ray, as well as Mel Blanc, the unforgettable magician of vocal effects. Nevertheless, despite their liveliness, the thirty-four animated cartoons produced by Chuck Jones are only a pale reflection of the early ones. In two instances—"Matinee Mouse" (1966) and "Shutter Bugged Cat" (1967)—Jones allowed Tom Ray to direct films with "reuse" of older productions.

Chuck Jones's name does not appear in the credits, which include the names of both William Hanna and Joseph Barbera, the older creators, as well as the newer men who did the transitional episodes in the older style.

The appearance in 1966 of "Matinee Mouse" between "Filet Meow" and "The A-Tom-Inable Snowman" really came as a sudden rejuvenation, with a revival of the former perfect line drawing and an animation that was full of ideas.

All this showed that the series was drawing to an end. During a time of financial difficulty, MGM was indeed forced to end the series. The very high production costs of the recent cartoons had exhausted the budget. They had produced 161 animated cartoons over a period of twenty-seven years. Tom and Jerry had been born in the year of *Rebecca* and *Waterloo Bridge.* They faded while Hollywood was producing *Bonnie and Clyde, Reflections in a Golden Eye, The Graduate,* and *In Cold Blood.* It was 1967.

Fred Quimby had died two years before, and Walt Disney, the preceding year, in 1966.

As victims of television's competition and the cost of standardized production, the Hollywood cartoons were frequently scheduled by the same television station. In 1975, William Hanna and Joseph Barbera revived Tom and Jerry on the ABC network by producing a series of new animated cartoons. Apart from the presence of a cat named Tom and a mouse named Jerry, every technical aspect of the cartoon short had been substantially changed. Tom and Jerry's golden age had concluded.

Tom and Jerry became television heros. . . .

A FASCINATING EXPERIENCE

Throughout seventeen years and 114 films (with the cartoons of Gene Deitch and of Chuck Jones forming two totally separate groups) the cartoons directed by William Hanna and Joseph Barbera proved to be a dazzling revelation. The point of departure was simple! A cat and a mouse. The cat sleeps in a basket, laps his daily milk, and tries to improve his diet by emptying the refrigerator. The mouse lives in a hole that is a veritable miniature house. A sardine tin is used as a bed. The chair is made of matchsticks, a demitasse cup becomes an armchair, and a thimble becomes a lamp. Hanna and Barbera had decided that this familiar framework would only occasionally be abandoned (Tom and Jerry turning up in the world of Robin Hood or in that of the French monarchy). They constantly enriched it by outside contributions. Mammy Two Shoes, Butch and Pup (Spike and Tyke), Nibbles (Tuffy), and the duckling all became supplementary characters without harming the cohesion of the couple formed by Tom and Jerry. An animal kingdom formed about them, made of magpie and the old horse, eagle and hen, lion and bull, goldfish and ant, frog and seal, elephant and tortoise, crab and shark.

Hanna and Barbera played upon the anthropomorphism of the two heroes and chose to give humans an even more minimal role than Walt Disney did. A faceless woman, Mammy Two Shoes, remained a character apart, and the absence of humans in all the first episodes of the series (with the exception of "Baby Puss," 1945) contributed to a mystery surrounding them. What was this house with no master in which Tom and Jerry lived? Mammy Two Shoes was obviously a maid and not the owner of the place. A couple did appear in 1954's "Pet Peeve" and then a mistress, either blond or brunette in the wake of the UPA cartoons, which stressed humans over animals. Seemingly simple and reassuring, the Tom and Jerry series of Hanna and Barbera raises a number of questions. "Was Jerry a female?" is one. The relationship of Tom and Jerry is very curious. It vacillates between hostility and friendship. The complicity of a latent love is carefully sustained by the ambiguity of Jerry's sex. The game between them evolves from teasing to violence. Despite the explosion of several hundred sticks of dynamite and bombs and innumerable blows of all sorts, the two characters keep—and this is in the tradition of the animated cartoon—the same appearance, as though nothing has happened to them. Whether he is cut to shreds, tonsured, crushed, flattened, shaved, or atomized, Tom, like the rising phoenix, remains the same.

In contrast to Tex Avery, who liked to use word play and references to history and to American life, Hanna and Barbera created a series of almost silent cartoons, with Tom and Jerry

"Solid Serenade" (1946)

38

exchanging no more than a few words in seventeen years. Still, Jerry can talk, as we have seen, and Tom, like Charles Boyer, murmurs sweet nothings to his ladylove and occasionally sings. Their creators didn't really use this ability, although its absence in no way harmed the effectiveness of the whole. As for Tex Avery, the sound, the noises, and the music—provided by Scott Bradley—created a sound environment that was dazzlingly rich. Without Scott Bradley and that perfect sound, Chuck Jones was reduced to using visual onomatopoeia (BAM! SOCKO!) in his series. The result was less convincing.

Tom, Jerry, Uncle Pecos (Jerry's singing and guitar-playing uncle), Tom's timid Cousin George, Jerry's athletic Cousin Muscles, Dreamboy, and a multitude of secondary characters meet and mix throughout this animated galaxy where anything is possible: the love of a mouse for a cat, the appearance of the guillotine under Louis XIII, the maddest metamorphoses, and the subtlest variations. This was the golden age of Hollywood's animated film—and of the cinema.

CHRONOLOGY 1940—1967

The Tom and Jerry series	MGM's other cartoons	Cartoons from other studios	The films	
1940 • **Puss Gets the Boot**	Twelve cartoons, including "The Fishing Bear" "The Homeless Flea" "Home on the Range" "Swing Social" "The Milky Way"	"Knock Knock" (WL) "The Mouse Exterminator" (Col) "Pluto's Dream House" (WD) "Cross Country Detours" (WB) "A Wild Hare" (WB) "Of Fox and Hounds" (WB) "Pinocchio" (WD) "Fantasia" (WD)	*The Grapes of Wrath* (Ford) *The Great Dictator* (Chaplin) *The Mark of Zorro* (Mamoulian) *The Mortal Storm* (Borzage) *The Philadelphia Story* (Cukor)	*Rebecca* (Hitchcock) *The Sea Hawk* (Curtiz) *The Shop Around the Corner* (Lubitsch) *Strange Cargo* (Borzage) *Waterloo Bridge* (LeRoy)
1941 • **The Midnight Snack** • **The Night Before Christmas**	Eleven cartoons, including "Abdul the Buibul Ameer" "Rookie Bear" "The Alley Cat" "Little Caesario" "The Field Mouse"	"What's Cookin'?" (WL) "The Crackpot Quail" (WB) "Porky's Preview" (WB) "Hollywood Steps Out" (WB) "The Bug Parade" (WB) "Hiawatha's Rabbit Hunt" (WB) "Rhapsody in Rivets" (WB) "Dumbo" (WD)	*Babies on Broadway* (Berkeley) *Citizen Kane* (Welles) *Dr. Jekyll and Mr. Hyde* (Fleming) *High Sierra* (Walsh)	*The Maltese Falcon* (Huston) *Sergeant York* (Hawks) *The Shanghai Gesture* (Von Sternberg) *Tarzan's Secret Treasure* (Thorpe) *They Died with Their Boots On* (Walsh)
1942 • **Fraidy Cat** • **Dog Trouble** • **Puss 'n' Toots** • **The Bowling Alley-Cat** • **Fine Feathered Friend**	Ten cartoons, including "The Bear and the Beavers" "Little Gravel Voice" "The Blitz Wolf" "The Earlt Bird Doot It" "Wild Honey"	"All Out for V" (WL) "A Hollywood Detour" (Col) "Toil Bridges Trouble" (Col) "The Wabbit Who Came to Supper" (WB) "My Favorite Duck" (WB) "Case of the Missing Hare" (WB) "You're a Sap, Mister Jap" (Par) "Mickey's Birthday Party" (WD) "Bambi" (WD)	*Casablanca* (Curtiz) *Cat People* (Tourneur) *Gentleman Jim* (Walsh) *The Magnificent Ambersons* (Welles) *The Moon and Six Pence* (Lewin)	*Mrs. Miniver* (Wyler) *Random Harvest* (LeRoy) *To Be or Not to Be* (Lubitsch) *Yankee Doodle Dandy* (Curtiz)
1943 • **Sufferin' Cats** • **The Lonesome Mouse** • **The Yankee Doodle Mouse** • **Baby Puss**	Ten cartoons, including "Dumbo Hounded" "Red Hot Riding Hood" "Who Killed Who?" "One Ham's Family" "What's Buzzin' Buzzard"	"The Dizzy Acrobat" (WL) "Imagination" (Col) "Pigs in a Polka" (WB) "Greetings Bait" (WB) "Daffy the Commando" (WB) "Der Fuehrer's Face" (WD) "Marry-Go-Round" (Par) "Saludos Amigos" (WD)	*Air Force* (Hawks) *Bataan* (Garnett) *Cry Havoc* (Thorpe) *For Whom the Bell Tolls* (Wood) *Heaven Can Wait* (Lubitsch) *Lassie Come Home* (McLeod Wilcox)	*Mission to Moscow* (Curtiz) *The Ox-Bow Incident* (Wellman) *Shadow of a Doubt* (Hitchcock) *The Song of Bernadette* (King)
1944 • **The Zoot Cat** • **The Million Dollar Cat** • **The Bodyguard** • **Puttin' On the Dog** • **Mouse Trouble**	Eight cartoons, including "Screwball Squirrel" "Batty Baseball" "Happy Go Nutty" "Big Heel Watha"	"Fish Fry" (WL) "What's Cookin', Doc?" (WB) "The Swooner Crooner" (WB) "Lulu in Hollywood" (Par)	*An American Romance* (Vidor) *Buffalo Bill* (Wellman) *Double Indemnity* (Wilder) *Gaslight* (Cukor) *Laura* (Preminger) *Meet Me in St. Louis* (Minnelli)	*The Story of Dr. Wassell* (De Mille) *To Have and Have Not* (Hawks) *Wilson* (King)
1945 • **The Mouse Comes to Dinner** • **Mouse in Manhattan** • **Tea for Two** • **Flirty Birdy** • **Quiet Please**	Six cartoons, including "Screwy Truant" "Shooting of Dan McGoo" "Swing Shift Cinderella" "Wild and Wolfy"	"Life with Feathers" (WB) "Shape Ahoy" (Par) "The Clock Watcher" (WD) "Gypsy Life" (TT) "The Three Caballeros" (WD)	*The Clock* (Minnelli) *Hangover Square* (Brahm) *Leave Her to Heaven* (Stahl) *Mildred Pierce* (Curtiz) *Objective Burma* (Walsh)	*The Picture of Dorian Gray* (Lewin) *Spellbound* (Hitchcock)
1946 • **Springtime for Thomas** • **The Milky Waif** • **Trap Happy** • **Solid Serenade**	Four cartoons, including "Lonesome Lenny" "Northwest Hounded Police"	"The Uninvited Pest" (TT) "The Poet and Peasant" (WL) "Hair Raising Hare" (WB) "Walky Talky Hawky" (WB) "The Big Snooze" (WB) "Klondike Casanova" (Par) "Song of the South" (WD)	*The Best Years of Our Lives* (Wyler) *The Big Sleep* (Hawks) *Dragonwyck* (Mankiewicz) *Gilda* (C. Vidor) *The Killers* (Siodmak)	*Notorious* (Hitchcock) *The Razor's Edge* (Goulding) *It's a Wonderful Life* (Capra) *The Postman Always Rings Twice* (Garnett) *My Darling Clementine* (Ford)

The Tom and Jerry series	MGM's other cartoons	Cartoons from other studios	The films	
1947 • **Cat Fishin'** • **Part Time Pal** • **The Cat Concerto** • **Dr. Jekyll and Mr. Mouse** • **Salt Water Tabby** • **A Mouse in the House** • **The Invisible Mouse**	Five cartoons, including "Hound Hunters" "Uncle Tom's Cabaña" "Slap Happy Lion" "King-Size Canary"	"Tweety Pie" (WB) "Birth of a Notion" (WB) "A Pest in the House" (WB) "Slick Hare" (WB) "Musica-Lulu" (Par) "Wotta Knight" (Par) "Chip 'n' Dale" (WD) "Pluto's Blue Note" (WD)	*Brute Force* (Dassin) *Duel in the Sun* (Vidor) *The Private Affairs of Bel Ami* (Lewin) *Secret Beyond the Door* (Lang) *Kiss of Death* (Hathaway)	*Forever Amber* (Preminger) *Lucy in the Lake* (Montgomery) *Pursued* (Walsh) *The Ghost and Mrs. Muir* (Mankiewicz) *Monsieur Verdoux* (Chaplin)
1948 • **Kitty Foiled** • **The Truce Hurts** • **Old Rockin' Chair Tom** • **Professor Tom** • **Mouse Cleaning**	Seven cartoons, including "The Bear and the Bean" "What Price Freedom" "Little Tinker" "Half-Pint Pigmy" "The Cat That Hated People"	"The Mad Hatter" (WL) "Buccaneer Bunny" (WB) "Haredevil Hare" (WB) "The Foghorn Leghorn" (WB) "Pre-Hysterical Man" (Par) "Mickey and the Seal" (WD) "Tea for Two Hundred" (WD) "Robin Hoodlum" (Upa)	*Key Largo* (Huston) *A Letter to Three Wives* (Mankiewicz) *They Live by Night* (Ray) *The Naked City* (Dassin) *Red River* (Hawks)	*The Lady from Shanghai* (Welles) *Three Godfathers* (Ford) *The Treasure of the Sierra Madre* (Huston) *The Pirate* (Minnelli) *The Three Musketeers* (Sidney)
1949 • **Polka-Dot Puss** • **The Little Orphan** • **Hatch Up Your Troubles** • **Heavenly Puss** • **The Cat and the Mermouse** • **Love That Pup** • **Jerry's Diary** • **Tennis Chumps**	Nine cartoons, including "Bad Luck Blackie" "Señor Droopy" "Little Rural Riding Hood" "Out-Foxed" "The Counterfeit Cat"	"Mouse Wreckers" (WB) "Daffy Duck Hunt" (WB) "For Scent-imental Reasons" (WB) "Lumber Jack and Jill" (Par) "Toy Tinkers" (WD) "Ragtime Bear" (Upa)	*All the King's Men* (Rossen) *Battleground* (Wellman) *The Fountainhead* (Vidor) *Gun Crazy* (Lewis) *Madame Bovary* (Minnelli) *The Step-up* (Wise) *She Wore a Yellow Ribbon* (Ford)	*Colorado Territory* (Walsh) *The Great Sinner* (Siodmak) *Intruder in the Dust* (Brown) *On the Town* (Kelly-Donen) *Samson and Delilah* (De Mille) *White Heat* (Walsh) *Twelve O'Clock High* (King)
1950 • **Little Quacker** • **Saturday Evening Puss** • **Texas Tom** • **Jerry and the Lion** • **Safety Second** • **Tom and Jerry in the Hollywood Bowl** • **The Framed Cat** • **Cueball Cat**	Five cartoons, including "Ventriloquist Cat" "The Cuckoo Clock" "Garden Gopher" "The Peachy Cobbler"	"Cat Happy" (TT) "Mutiny on the Bunny" (WB) "What's Up, Doc?" (WB) "Canary Row" (WB) "Rabbit of Seville" (WB) "Beach Peach" (Par) "Popeye Makes a Movie" (Par) "Trouble Indemnity" (Upa) "Cinderella" (WD)	*All About Eve* (Mankiewicz) *Broken Arrow* (Daves) *The Gunfighter* (King) *King Solomon's Mines* (Marton-Bennett) *Sunset Boulevard* (Wilder) *Winchester 73* (Mann)	*The Asphalt Jungle* (Huston) *Devil's Doorway* (Mann) *House by the River* (Lang) *Stars in My Crown* (Tourneur) *Three Little Words* (Thorpe)
1951 • **Casanova Cat** • **Jerry and the Goldfish** • **Jerry's Cousin** • **Sleepy-Time Tom** • **His Mouse Friday** • **Slicked-Up Pup** • **Nit-Witty Kitty** • **Cat Napping**	Six cartoons, including "Cock-a-Doodle Dog" "Daredevil Droopy" "Symphony in Slang"	"Sleep Happy" (WL) "Tweet, Tweet, Tweety" (WB) "One Quack Mind" (Par) "Drippy Mississippi" (Par) "Gerald McBoing Boing" (Upa) "Alice in Wonderland" (WD)	*Across the Wide Missouri* (Wellman) *The Big Carnival* (Wilder) *People Will Talk* (Mankiewicz) *The Red Badge of Courage* (Huston) *A Streetcar Named Desire* (Kazan) *Westward the Woman* (Wellman)	*An American in Paris* (Minnelli) *The Day the Earth Stood Still* (Wise) *The Prowler* (Losey) *Strangers on a Train* (Hitchcock) *Vengeance Valley* (Thorpe)
1952 • **The Flying Cat** • **The Duck Doctor** • **The Two Mouseketeers** • **Smitten Kitten** • **Triplet Trouble** • **Little Runaway** • **Fit to Be Tied** • **Push-Button Kitty** • **Cruise Cat** • **The Dog House**	Six cartoons, including "Magical Maestro" "Rock-a-Bye Bear"	"Termites from Mars" (WL) "Operation: Rabbit" (WB) "Hasty Hare" (WB) "Popeye's Pappy" (Par) "Lambert the Sheepish Lion" (WD) "Rooty Toot Toot" (Upa) "Pink and Blue Blues" (Upa) "Madeline" (Upa)	*Bend of the River* (Mann) *Deadline-U.S.A.* (Brooks) *High Noon* (Zinnemann) *Ivanhoe* (Thorpe) *The Prisoner of Zenda* (Thorpe) *Scaramouche* (Sidney) *Viva Zapata* (Kazan)	*The Big Sky* (Hawks) *Five Fingers* (Mankiewicz) *The Iron Mistress* (Douglas) *Limelight* (Chaplin) *The Quiet Man* (Ford) *Singin' in the Rain* (Kelly-Donen)
1953 • **The Missing Mouse** • **Jerry and Jumbo** • **Johann Mouse** • **That's My Pup** • **Just Ducky** • **Two Little Indians** • **Life with Tom**	Eight cartoons, including "Little Johnny Jet" "Wee Willie Wildcat" "Three Little Pups"	"Rugged Bear" (WD) "Snow Business" (WB) "Tom-Tom Tomcat" (WB) "Duck, Rabbit, Duck" (WB) "Frightday the 13th" (Par) "Christopher Crumpet" (Upa) "Toot, Whistle, Plunk and Boom" (WD) "Peter Pan" (WD)	*The Bad and the Beautiful* (Minnelli) *From Here to Eternity* (Zinnemann) *The Naked Spur* (Mann) *Mogambo* (Ford) *Julius Caesar* (Mankiewicz) *The Band Wagon* (Minnelli)	*The Big Heat* (Lang) *Lili* (Walters) *Pick Up on South Street* (Fuller) *Niagara* (Hathaway) *All the Brothers Were Valiant* (Thorpe) *Battle Circus* (Brooks)

The Tom and Jerry series	MGM's other cartoons	Cartoons from other studios	The films	
1954 • Puppy Tale • Posse Cat • Hic-Cup Pup • Little School Mouse • Baby Butch • Mice Follies • Neapolitan Mouse • Downhearted Duckling • Pet Peeve • Touché, Pussy Cat	Nine cartoons, including "Drag-Along Droopy" "Billy Boy" "The Flea Circus"	"I'm Cold" (WL) "Captain Hareblower" (WB) "Satan's Waitin' " (WB) "Gopher Spinach" (Par) "Destination Magoo" (Upa) "Pigs Is Pigs" (WD) "From A to Z-Z-Z-Z" (WB) "Boo Moon" (Par)	*The Adventures of Hajji Baba* (Weis) *The Barefoot Contessa* (Mankiewicz) *Executive Suite* (Wise) *Knights of the Round Table* (Thorpe) *Brigadoon* (Minnelli) *Johnny Guitar* (Ray) *River of No Return* (Preminger)	*Apache* (Aldrich) *Rear Window* (Hitchcock) *Give a Girl a Break* (Donen) *On the Waterfront* (Kazan) *The Garden of Evil* (Hathaway) *The Long Long Trailer* (Minnelli) *Rogue Cop* (Rowland)
1955 • Southbound Duckling • Pup on a Picnic • Mouse for Sale • Designs on Jerry • Tom and Cherie • Smarty Cat • Pecos Pest • That's My Mommy	Five cartoons, including "Field and Scream" "Deputy Droopy"	"Crazy Mixed-Up Pup" (WL) "The Legend of Rockabye Point" (WL) "Sandy Claws" (WB) "Speedy Gonzales" (WB) "When Magoo Flew" (Upa) "Magoo Makes News" (Upa) "Lady and the Tramp" (WD)	*Blackboard Jungle* (Brooks) *East of Eden* (Kazan) *Kiss Me Deadly* (Aldrich) *Moonfleet* (Lang) *The Seven Year Itch* (Wilder) *Violent Saturday* (Fleischer)	*The Cobweb* (Minnelli) *House of Bamboo* (Fuller) *Love Is a Many Splendored Thing* (King) *The Night of the Hunter* (Laughton) *Rebel Without a Cause* (Ray)
1956 • The Flying Sorceress • The Egg and Jerry • Busy Buddies • Muscle Beach Tom • Downbeat Bear • Blue Cat Blues • Barbecue Brawl	One cartoon "Millionaire Droopy"	"Calling All Cuckoos" (WL) "Rocket Squad" (WB) "A Star Is Bored" (WB) "Popeye for President" (Par) "In the Bag" (WD) "Hooked Bear" (WD) "Gerald McBoing Boing on the Planet Moo" (Upa) "Magoo's Puddle Jumper" (Upa)	*Forbidden Planet* (McLeod Wilcox) *The Searchers* (Ford) *The Ten Commandments* (De Mille) *Ransom* (Segal)	*The Last Hunt* (Brooks) *Seven Men from Now* (Boetticher) *Somebody Up There Likes Me* (Wise) *The Man Who Knew Too Much* (Hitchcock)
1957 • Tops with Pops • Timid Tabby • Feedin' the Kiddie • Mucho Mouse • Tom's Photo Finish	Six cartoons, including "Blackboard Jumble" "One Droopy Knight"	"Flebus" (TT) "Tabasco Road" (WB) "Birds Anonymous" (WB) "Rabbit Romeo" (WB) "Hooky Spooky" (Par) "The Truth about Mother Goose" (WD) "Matador Magoo" (Upa)	*Band of Angels* (Walsh) *Designing Woman* (Minnelli) *Run of the Arrow* (Fuller) *A Face in the Crowd* (Kazan) *Something of Value* (Brooks)	*The Wings of Eagles* (Ford) *Written on the Wind* (Sirk) *The Sun Also Rises* (King) *Jailhouse Rock* (Thorpe)
1958 • Happy Go Ducky • Royal Cat Nap • The Vanishing Duck • Robin Hoodwinked • Tot Watchers	Three cartoons, including "Mutts about Racing" "Droopy Leprechaun"	"Sidney's Family Tree" (TT) "Watch the Birdie" (WL) "Knighty-Knight Bugs" (WB) "Cat Feud" (WB) "Ghost Writers" (Par) "Paul Bunyan" (WD) "Trees and Jamaica Daddy" (Upa)	*Cat on a Hot Tin Roof* (Brooks) *Gigi* (Minnelli) *Party Girl* (Ray) *A Time to Love and a Time to Die* (Sirk) *Man of the West* (Mann)	*Cry Terror* (Stone) *The Left Handed Gun* (Penn) *Touch of Evil* (Welles) *Vertigo* (Hitchcock) *The Last Hurrah* (Ford)
1959	None	"China Jones" (WB) "Wild and Wooly Hare" (WB) "Tweet Dreams" (WB) "Donald in Mathmagic Land" (WD) "Magoo's Homecoming" (Upa) "Sleeping Beauty" (WD) "1001 Arabian Nights" (Upa)	*Imitation of Life* (Sirk) *Some Like It Hot* (Wilder) *Rio Bravo* (Hawks) *Warlock* (Dmytryk) *Ben Hur* (Wyler)	*North by Northwest* (Hitchcock) *Some Came Running* (Minnelli) *The World, the Flesh and the Devil* (MacDougall)
1960	None	"House of Hashimoto" (TT) "Mouse and Garden" (WB) "Horse Hare" (WB) "High Note" (WB)	*Exodus* (Preminger) *Elmer Gantry* (Brooks) *Home from the Hill* (Minnelli) *The Subterraneans* (MacDougall)	*Psycho* (Hitchcock) *Strangers When We Meet* (Quine) *Spartacus* (Kubrick) *The Time Machine* (Pal)
1961 • Switchin' Kitten • Down and Outing • It's Greek to Me-Ow	None	"The Pied Piper of Guadalupe" (WB) "Beep Prepared" (WB) "Nelly's Folly" (WB) "Bopin'Hood" (Par) "One Hundred and One Dalmatians" (WD)	*The Errand Boy* (Lewis) *Splendor in the Grass* (Kazan) *The Misfits* (Huston) *One-Eyed Jacks* (Brando)	*The Hustler* (Rossen) *The Last Sunset* (Aldrich) *West Side Story* (Wise-Robbins)

The Tom and Jerry series	MGM's other cartoons	Cartoons from other studios	The films	
1962 • **High Steaks** • **Mouse into Space** • **Landing Stripling** • **Calypso Cat** • **Dicky Moe** • **The Tom and Jerry Cartoon Kit** • **Tall in the Trap** • **Sorry Safari** • **Buddies Thicker Than Water** • **Carmen Get It!**	None	"Rock-a-Bye Gator" (WL) "A Sheep in the Deep" (WB) "Wet Hare" (WB) "Frogs Legs" (Par) "Gay Purr-ee" (Upa)	*Advise and Consent* (Preminger) *Hatari!* (Hawks) *The Man Who Shot Liberty Valance* (Ford) *Sweet Bird of Youth* (Brooks)	*The Four Horsemen of the Apocalypse* (Minnelli) *Ride the High Country* (Peckinpah) *Two Weeks in Another Town* (Minnelli)
1963 • **Penthouse Mouse**	None	"Now Hear This" (WB) "Transylvania 6-5000" (WB) "To Beep or Not to Beep" (WB) "Harry Happy" (Par) "Sword in the Stone" (WD)	*The Birds* (Hitchcock) *The Courtship of Eddie's Father* (Minnelli)	*Cleopatra* (Mankiewicz) *The Nutty Professor* (Lewis)
1964 • **The Cat Above and the Mouse Below** • **Is There a Doctor in the Mouse?** • **Much Ado About Mousing** • **Snowbody Loves Me** • **The Unshrinkable Jerry Mouse**	None	"The Case of the Maltese Chicken" (WL) "Dumb Patrol" (WB) "Freudy Cat" (WB) "Accidents Will Happen" (Par)	*Lilith* (Rossen) *Marnie* (Hitchcock) *Seven Days in May* (Frankenheimer)	*Cheyenne Autumn* (Ford) *My Fair Lady* (Cukor) *Viva Las Vegas* (Sidney)
1965 • **Ah, Sweet Mouse-Story of Life** • **Tom-Ic Energy** • **Bad Day at Cat Rock** • **The Brothers Carry-Mouse-Off** • **Haunted Mouse** • **I'm Just Wild About Jerry** • **Of Feline Bondage** • **The Year of the Mouse** • **The Cat's Me–Ouch** • **Jerry-Go-Round**	One cartoon	"Three Little Woodpeckers" (WL) "The Wild Chase" (WB) "Moby Duck" (WB) "Tease for Two" (WB)	*Major Dundee* (Peckinpah) *The Sandpiper* (Minnelli) *The Cincinnati Kid* (Jewison)	*Bus Riley's Back in Town* (Hart) *The Sons of Katie Elder* (Hathaway)
1966 • **Duel Personality** • **Jerry, Jerry Quite Contrary** • **Love Me, Love My Mouse** • **Puss 'n' Boats** • **Filet Meow** • **Matinee Mouse** • **The A-Tom-Inable Snowman** • **Catty Cornered**	None	"Mucho Locos" (WB) "Sugar and Spies" (WB) "Winnie the Pooh and the Honey Tree" (WD)	*The Chase* (Penn) *The Professionals* (Brooks)	*The Group* (Lumet) *Seven Women* (Ford)
1967 • **Cat and Dupli-Cat** • **O-Solar Meow** • **Guided Mouse-ille** • **Rock 'n' Rodent** • **Cannery Rodent** • **The Mouse from H.U.N.G.E.R.** • **Surf-Bored Cat** • **Shutter Bugged Cat** • **Advance and Be Mechanized** • **Purr Chance to Dream**	One cartoon	"Daffy's Diner" (WB) "The Quacker Tracker" (WB) "The Music Mice-tro" (WB) "The Jungle Book" (WD)	*Bonnie and Clyde* (Penn) *El Dorado* (Hawks) *Reflections in a Golden Eye* (Huston)	*The Dirty Dozen* (Aldrich) *The Last Challenge* (Thorpe)

(WL) Walter Lantz
(Col) Columbia
(WD) Walt Disney
(WB) Warner Bros.
(Par) Paramount
(TT) Terrytoons
(Upa) United Productions of America

1940

PUSS GETS THE BOOT

Directors: William Hanna,
Joseph Barbera
Producer: Rudolf Ising
(Metro-Goldwyn-Mayer)
Animation: Carl Urbano, Tony Pabian,
Jack Zander, Pete Burness, Bob Allen
Music: Scott Bradley
Technicolor (9 min. 15 sec.)

Jerry tries to escape Tom, who swallows him with the greatest of ease. Tom paints a fake mouse hole in the wall. Jerry crashes into it and is knocked out. Tom revives him, and during the ensuing chase knocks over a vase of flowers. The noise attracts the black maid, who threatens to put Tom out if he continues.

Jerry takes a glass and acts as if he will break it, throwing it up in the air. Tom catches it. Jerry continues to throw the dishes up in the air, but Tom manages to get his paws on Jerry, and amuses himself with taunting him, like a cat with a mouse. Jerry lets the dishes fall, and Tom gives up catching them. Jerry takes advantage of the situation to bathe in Tom's saucer of milk. He dries himself with the unfortunate cat's tail. Tom then slaps Jerry's behind with his paw, causing the pile of dishes to fall. Tom is put outdoors, and Jerry enjoys his triumph.

Notes

• **William Hanna and Joseph Barbera, the film's directors, are not listed in the credits. Only Rudolf Ising is credited.**

• **The cat is really called Jasper, not Tom. The name of Tom (Thomas) was a later substitution.**

• **The black maid calls Jasper/Tom "you good-for-nothin' cheap fur coat." This is the first of Mammy Two Shoes' eighteen appearances.**

• **The film was nominated for the Academy Award.**

1941

THE MIDNIGHT SNACK

Direction: William Hanna,
Joseph Barbera
Producer: Fred Quimby
(Metro-Goldwyn-Mayer)
Music: Scott Bradley
Technicolor (8 min. 15 sec.)

Jerry steals a piece of Swiss cheese from the refrigerator. Tom catches him and piles heavy objects on top of the cheese. Jerry finally slips on a rolling pin and falls. He brings the Swiss cheese back to the refrigerator. Tom stuffs himself, while Jerry, caught behind an iron, is reduced to meditating on his bad luck. Tom throws the piece of cheese away and breaks the dishes.

The black maid appears, and Tom puts Jerry inside the refrigerator. The maid, frightened on discovering Jerry's presence, calls Tom to her aid. But Jerry manages to wedge Tom in behind the ironing board.

Using a fork Jerry projects Tom into the sink, onto the grater, and finally into the refrigerator, which shuts behind him. The maid is scandalized to discover Tom in the emptied refrigerator. She chases him out, while Jerry is free—at last—to eat his piece of Swiss cheese.

Notes

• **Musical score: "Sing Before Breakfast" (Brown)**

• **William Hanna, Joseph Barbera, and Fred Quimby appear together for the first time in the credits of a Tom and Jerry. The celebrated trio is now formed!**

1 9 4 1

THE NIGHT BEFORE CHRISTMAS

Direction: William Hanna, Joseph
Barbera (Metro-Goldwyn-Mayer)
Animation: Kenneth Muse, Jack
Zander, Pete Burness
Technicolor (8 min. 47 sec.)

It's Christmas Eve, and the tree is decorated. Jerry discovers a Swiss cheese present on a threatening trap. He sees his
reflection on one of the Christmas tree or-
naments, and jumps from one gift to another. He jumps onto a plush lion, then onto
. . . Tom. Tom gets excited, but gives himself
an electric shock while trying to grab hold
of Jerry, who escapes onto a toy train, but
falls off at the entry tunnel. Jerry hides in a
glove box, and hits Tom.

The cat gets into a rage, but Jerry waves
a branch of mistletoe and pretends to kiss
him. Tom starts to play the lover, but Jerry
hits him over the head. Tom chases him, and
Jerry escapes from the house through the
opening of the mail slot. Tom immediately
blocks it.

He then goes over to sleep peacefully by
the fire while Jerry, outside wanders
through the cold, under the snow. Tom
takes pity on him and lets him in, but Jerry
is frozen. Tom attends to him and defrosts
him. Jerry then carries off the mousetrap
lying near Tom's bowl. He retrieves his
cheese gift, and discovers that the mouse
trap was really a kind of music box.

Note
- **The film was nominated for an Academy Award.**

1942

FRAIDY CAT

Directors: William Hanna,
Joseph Barbera
Producer: Fred Quimby
(Metro-Goldwyn-Mayer)
Music: Scott Bradley
Technicolor (8 min. 11 sec.)

Tom is frightened as he listens to "The Witching Hour," a radio serial. Shivers run up and down his spine. Jerry enjoys making fun of him. He rattles a window shade, then swells up a blouse with a vacuum cleaner. Tom thinks he sees a ghost and faints dead away. Jerry revives him and starts his diabolical tricks again. The vacuum cleaner begins to swallow up everything in sight. Tom hangs onto the staircase while his lives—his "nine lives"—are sucked up by the machine.

Tom finally discovers the truth, and the cause of his fright. He chases Jerry, but collides with an ashtray and is knocked out. The black maid arrives, armed with a rolling pin. Tom bites her, thinking she is Jerry disguised as a ghost.

Jerry disguises himself as a white mouse but is scared, in turn, by the sight of his own giant reflection.

DOG TROUBLE

Directors: William Hanna,
Joseph Barbera
Producer: Fred Quimby
(Metro-Goldwyn-Mayer)
Music: Scott Bradley
Technicolor (7 min. 57 sec.)

Tom is chasing Jerry. Jerry puts Tom's tail in the mousetrap. Tom continues to chase Jerry and runs into Bulldog (Spike). Bulldog begins to chase Tom. Jerry finds the situation amusing until he, in turn, is chased by Bulldog. Tom hangs onto the lamp and Jerry onto the cuckoo clock, and both manage to escape Bulldog's fangs. Jerry manages to save Tom, who was about to fall.

A few moments later, Jerry falls and Tom manages, in the nick of time, to snatch him from Bulldog's jaws. Tom and Jerry shake hands and form a plan to get rid of Bulldog. Tom eggs him on, Jerry taunts and provokes him. Bulldog can't catch Tom, who is clinging to the clock. Meanwhile, Jerry lays a cord down through the house. Bulldog fol-

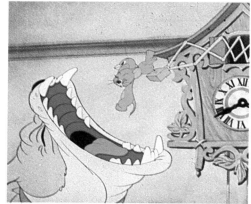

lows it, and, finding himself soon entrapped, breaks up the entire house. The black maid puts him out.

Tom and Jerry enjoy their victory, but Tom gets his tail caught in the mousetrap and, now furious, he set off in pursuit of Jerry.

Note

• This marks the first appearance of the dog who, as Spike or Butch, will be either friend or foe, depending upon the episode. Here he is really aggressive, howling, and savagely attacks both Tom and Jerry. Confronted with this violent enemy, they unite in mutual assistance.

PUSS 'N' TOOTS

Directors: William Hanna,
Joseph Barbera
Producer: Fred Quimby
(Metro-Goldwyn-Mayer)
Music: Scott Bradley
Technicolor (7 min. 48 sec.)

Tom is amusing himself with Jerry, pushing him down inside an empty jar. The maid opens the door, and leaves a white kitten to be cared for. Tom immediately falls in love. He primps, and is transformed into a libidinous wolf.

Tom offers the kitten a fish, then a canary, and casually catches hold of Jerry, on whom he proceeds to play tricks. He makes him disappear and descent in a parachute. Jerry, now enraged, avenges himself by pricking Tom's behind. Tom is caught in an automatic record player, and his appearance changes according to the music being played. Tom, still caught, is knocked out by the machine.

Jerry, rid of his rival, primps in turn and gives the white cat a kiss before reentering his hole.

Note

• Musical score: "Sweet and Lovely" (Arnheim), "Darktown Strutters' Ball" (Brooks), "Horses" (Gay), "Boola Boola" (Hirsh), "Tiger Rag" (La Rocca).

THE BOWLING ALLEY-CAT

Directors: William Hanna,
Joseph Barbera
Producer: Fred Quimby
(Metro-Goldwyn-Mayer)
Music: Scott Bradley
Technicolor (8 min.)

Jerry is "skating" in a bowling alley when Tom appears. Jerry hurls him onto the alley. Tom crashes into an ashtray and is covered with ashes. Tom attempts to bowl, but falls on the backswing. He finally sends a series of balls toward Jerry, who manages to get out of their path. Tom, however, is caught by them. Tom gets hold of Jerry and the ball under his paw. Jerry attaches Tom to the ball by his tail. Tom runs, and the ball knocks him over, hitting him regularly. He is finally hurled outside, and Jerry, the delighted victor, marks down his winning score.

FINE FEATHERED FRIEND

Directors: William Hanna,
Joseph Barbera
Producer: Fred Quimby
(Metro-Goldwyn-Mayer)
Animation: Kenneth Muse, Pete Burness, George Gordon, Jack Zander, Bill Littlejohn
Music: Scott Bradley
Technicolor (7 min. 43 sec.)

Tom is chasing Jerry, who takes shelter under a hen. Tom catches up, but the hen chases him away. Jerry again takes shelter under the hen, but Tom, thinking he's got a hold on Jerry, actually takes an egg. The hen sends him running. Tom gets his tail caught in a mousetrap instead of catching Jerry. Discovering this, he screams in pain. The hen mounts on Tom's back and spurs him on with a fork.

The chicks hatch. Jerry disguises himself as a chick and mixes with them. Trying to catch Jerry, Tom steals a chick. The chick screams, and the hen arrives and knocks Tom out. Jerry slides in among some ducklings who have just crossed the row of chicks. He almost drowns. Tom cuts the hen's tail, and she takes revenge by cutting up Tom's tail.

Jerry snuggles up to sleep against the hen amid the chicks.

Notes
- **Musical score: "Horses" (Gay), "Tiger Rag" (Original Dixieland Jazz Band).**
- **A clever idea: the hen puts her eggs in order with a billiard triangle!**

SUFFERIN' CATS!

Directors: William Hanna,
Joseph Barbera
Producer: Fred Quimby
(Metro-Goldwyn-Mayer)
Animation: Kenneth Muse, George
Gordon, Pete Burness, Jack Zander
Music: Scott Bradley
Technicolor (7 min. 50 sec.)

Tom is casting a fishing rod to catch Jerry. Jerry collides with a dark alley cat, but immediately apologizes. Tom and the alley cat start threatening each other. The alley cat tries to make a sandwich snack of Jerry, but the mouse is ejected (by the pepper). Jerry pretends to be Tom's ally, and causes the two cats to fight. Tom attaches the alley cat's tail to a garden hose, but falls into a trash can while doing so. Jerry knocks Tom out with a hose. Pursued by the two cats, Jerry, disguised as an old, bearded mouse, ties the two cats together.

Jerry scatters tacks on the ground, and the two cats prick their paws. The cats then decide to cut Jerry in two and share him. But Tom's evil self tells him to eliminate his rival and keep Jerry to himself. So Tom finally strikes the alley cat, who strikes back. The two cats chase Jerry, and get caught in the door. Jerry takes advantage of this situation to beat up his two enemies with a wooden slat.

Note
- **Musical score: "Wonderful One" (Whiteman–Grofe).**

THE LONESOME MOUSE

Directors: William Hanna,
Joseph Barbera
Producer: Fred Quimby
(Metro-Goldwyn-Mayer)
Music: Scott Bradley
Technicolor (8 min. 7 sec.)

Tom is sleeping. Jerry breaks a vase on him. The black maid is furious over the broken vase and puts Tom out, accusing him of having done the deed. Jerry dances for joy; he is finally rid of Tom. He takes a swim in Tom's milk bowl, gives Tom's picture a Hitler mustache, and spits in the picture's face. He tears Tom's basket apart, and suddenly discovers that without his usual opponent, he's bored. So he goes outside to see him, frightening the maid by making faces at her. The maid then calls brave Tom to her rescue. He and Jerry pretend to fight and to chase each other. They share a piece of chicken, make music together, and, armed with knife and fork, fight a duel. Tom chases Jerry with a chopping blade, cutting up the table and making a mess of the whole house. The maid has had enough. Tom fools her into believing that he's finally gotten rid of Jerry. The maid feeds Tom, but Jerry arrives and eats Tom's food. Tom chases him away. Jerry, now angry, pushes him into the plate of food and calls him a fake.

Notes

- **Musical score: "Happy Days Are Here Again" (Ager), "Ach Du Lieber Augustin" (arr. Scott Bradley), "I Cried for You" (Freed et al.), "How About You?" (Lane–Freed), "Sing Before Breakfast Drums" (Brown–Freed).**

- **Jerry's drawing a Hitler-style mustache on Tom's picture is one of the very rare political allusions (the date is 1943) in the Tom and Jerry series.**

- **The style of drawing makes Tom look less hairy and more "modern" than in the preceding cartoons. This is no longer the "old Tom" of the series' early films.**

1 9 4 3

THE YANKEE DOODLE MOUSE

Directors: William Hanna,
Joseph Barbera
Producer: Fred Quimby
(Metro-Goldwyn-Mayer)
Animation: Irven Spence, Pete
Burness, Kenneth Muse, George
Gordon
Music: Scott Bradley
Technicolor (7 min. 23 sec.)

Tom is chasing Jerry, who hides in an anticat shelter. He launches egg grenades at Tom and bombards him with champagne bottle corks. Tom, hit by a cork, collapses into a tub of water. First military communiqué: "Sighted cat. Sank Same. Signed: Lieutenant Jerry Mouse." Jerry catches sight of Tom with his periscope, and attacks him with a grater mounted on a skate. Capsized, it stirs up a cloud of smoke and strikes Tom. Tom throws a stick of dynamite at Jerry, who returns it to him and gets it back again. They keep passing the stick back and forth to each other; then each tries to get it back. The stick explodes in Tom's face. Another stick of dynamite explodes in Tom's hands. This last stick breaks into successive pieces, leaving only a last little stick, which no longer worries Tom, but of course suddenly explodes, causing a lot of damage.

Jerry bombards Tom with light bulbs. Tom shoots down Jerry, who slows his fall using a brassiere as a parachute.

Jerry, with fireworks at his heels, directs them toward Tom. Tom ties him to some dynamite, which is attached to a ramp, but it is Tom who's shot into the sky. As the dynamite explodes, an American flag appears in the sky. Final communiqué: "Send more Cats. Signed: Lieutenant Jerry Mouse."

Notes

• **Musical score: "Over There" (Cohan), "Anchors Aweigh" (Zimmerman).**

• **The film won the Oscar for the best cartoon of 1943.**

• **This film is reused in "Jerry's Diary" (1949) and "Shutter Bugged Cat" (1967).**

• **The title clearly alludes to *Yankee Doodle Dandy* (1942), directed by Michael Curtiz, in which James Cagney plays George M. Cohan, the songwriter of "Over There."**

• **According to Mark Kausler, Irven Spence was responsible for the action and Kenneth Muse for the facial expressions.**

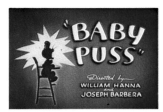

Baby Puss

Directors: William Hanna,
Joseph Barbera
Producer: Fred Quimby
(Metro-Goldwyn-Mayer)
Animation: Kenneth Muse, Ray
Patterson, Irven Spence, Pete Burness
Music: Scott Bradley
Technicolor (7 min. 51 sec.)

A little girl is playing with Tom as if he were a doll. Tom, left alone, behaves like a baby with a bottle. Jerry makes fun of him and, when chased, hides inside his house. Tom eyes Jerry inside his mouse house while he's taking a bath. Upon discovering the intruder, Jerry begins to scream. Jerry, dressed in a skirt like a doll, comes out of his house. Tom discovers the truth; it's really Jerry! He then destroys Jerry's house, but the little girl returns and puts Tom to bed again, threatening him with a dose of castor oil.

Jerry calls on three alley cats, who arrive and make fun of Tom. The three cats toss Tom to each other. They throw him into the aquarium, powder him, and put a fish in his diaper. The three cats sing "Mama, Mama, Mama, yo quiero." The smallest of the three sings and dances like Carmen Miranda.

The little girl returns. The three cats take to their heels, and the little girl gives Tom a dose of castor oil. Tom runs off to throw up. Jerry starts to laugh, and it's now his turn to absorb the castor oil. He, too, goes off to throw up.

Note
- Musical score: "You Must Have Been a Beautiful Baby" (Warren), "How About You?" (Lane–Freed), "Baby Face" (Davis–Akst), "Mama, Yo Quiero" (Jaraica–Paiva).

1944

THE ZOOT CAT

Directors: William Hanna,
Joseph Barbera
Producer: Fred Quimby
(Metro-Goldwyn-Mayer)
Animation: Ray Patterson, Kenneth
Muse, Irven Spence, Pete Burness
Music: Scott Bradley
Technicolor (7 min. 3 sec.)

Tom presents Jerry as a gift, all tied up in ribbons, to his girlfriend, a young black kitten. He sings and dances for her. The kitten insults him and returns his gift. Tom hears someone talking about the "zoot suit" on the radio. He grabs a lamp shade, cuts up a hammock, and appears before the amazed kitten as a real seducer.

Tom and the kitten, now under his spell, dance together. Tom sits down at the piano and begins talking to the kitten in the voice of Charles Boyer, but Jerry comes in and puts matches between Tom's toes, setting fire to them. Tom falls through a trap door. Jerry begins dancing with the kitten, but Tom reappears. Jerry attaches him to the window blind, and Tom is catapulted into a fish bowl. His suit shrinks, falls off, and now fits Jerry like a glove.

Notes

• **Musical score: "You Gotta See Mommy Every Night" (Rose–Conrad), "Honey" (Gillespie), "I'm a Ding Dong Daddy" (Baxter), "Elmer's Tune" (Albrecht), "The Chase" (Bradley), "Jersey Bounce" (Plater), "China Boy" (Boutelle–Winfrey), "Deep Purple" (Derose).**

• **Tom talks to his ladylove in the voice and accent of Charles Boyer, a tradition of the Tex Avery cartoons.**

• **According to Mark Kausler, Irven Spence worked especially on the jitterbugging sequence.**

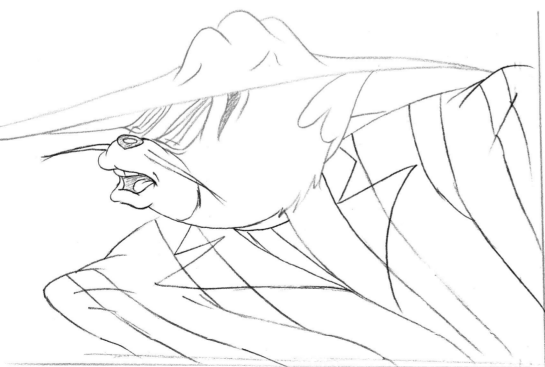

THE MILLION DOLLAR CAT

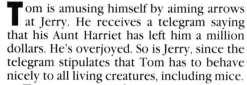

Directors: William Hanna,
Joseph Barbera
Producer: Fred Quimby
(Metro-Goldwyn-Mayer)
Animation: Irven Spence, Kenneth
Muse, Pete Burness, Ray Patterson
Music: Scott Bradley
Technicolor (7 min. 10 sec.)

Tom is amusing himself by aiming arrows at Jerry. He receives a telegram saying that his Aunt Harriet has left him a million dollars. He's overjoyed. So is Jerry, since the telegram stipulates that Tom has to behave nicely to all living creatures, including mice.

Tom, now very rich, moves to 1 Park Avenue, while Jerry lives at ½ Park Avenue.

Jerry sets about provoking Tom, who can do nothing, for fear of losing his fortune. Tom goes home, but finds Jerry there, devouring a cake meant for Tom. Tom locks Jerry up, but the mouse escapes and settles into bed, next to Tom.

Tom pretends there is a fire. Jerry, terrified, jumps out the window and into the void, but Tom can't get rid of him, and Jerry devours Tom's breakfast, as the cat's eyes pop out of their sockets.

Tom attacks Jerry, declaring, with satisfaction, "I've thrown a million dollars to the winds, but I'm happy!"

Note
• Musical score: "Boola Boola" (Hirsch), "Broadway Rhythm" (Brown), "Day Break" (Grofe), "Sing Before Breakfast" (Brown), "Sleepy Time Gal" (Whiting), "Thank You for a Lovely Evening" (McHugh), "Happy Days Are Here Again" (Ager).

THE BODYGUARD

Directors: William Hanna,
Joseph Barbera
Producer: Fred Quimby
(Metro-Goldwyn-Mayer)
Animation: Kenneth Muse, Pete
Burness, Ray Patterson, Irven Spence
Music: Scott Bradley
Technicolor (7 min. 21 sec.)

Spike the dog, who has just been captured by the pound, is set free by Jerry. In gratitude, the dog tells him, "If you're ever in need, just whistle; I'm your pal for life."

Tom grabs hold of Jerry and makes a sandwich of him. Jerry whistles. Spike dashes to Jerry's rescue and transforms Tom into an accordion. Jerry has a good time taunting Tom and then whistling, which immediately brings Spike onto the scene. Tom catches Jerry and prevents him from whistling, but suddenly he spies a little white kitten passing by and it's he who now whistles, in admiration. That's all that's needed to produce an immediate—and violent—response from Spike, alerted by the whistle.

Jerry chews some gum prepared by Tom and is no longer able to whistle. He tries in

PUTTIN' ON THE DOG

Directors: William Hanna,
Joseph Barbera
Producer: Fred Quimby
(Metro-Goldwyn-Mayer)
Animation: Pete Burness, Ray
Patterson, Irven Spence, Kenneth
Muse
Music: Scott Bradley
Technicolor (7 min. 2 sec.)

Tom chases Jerry and ends up in the dog pound. He escapes, while Jerry relaxes nonchalantly on Spike's head. Tom puts on a dog's head and passes for one. He sees Spike and begins to yelp. But Jerry, who also begins yelping, threatens Tom. Tom chases him and goes looking for him among the dogs. Spike threatens Tom, who is soon buried under a Saint Bernard. He escapes and hides in a barrel, where Jerry has already taken shelter.

Jerry hides in the hairy pelt of a big dog. Tom, in turn, plunges into the dog's pelt and appears before Spike without his dog face. Tom, trying to retrieve his mask, "pulls" on a real dog. Tom attacks Spike, believing he's Jerry. He runs away, then catches up with Jerry and puts on his mask again when Spike arrives. Tom, trying to knock Spike out, hits Jerry. The mouse shows Spike a hand-written sign, "Yes, stupid, it's a cat." Spike at last understands and chases Tom, with some of his fellow dogs at his side. Tom ends up on top of a mast, kept at bay by the dogs.

vain to explain the situation to Spike, who's content to reassure him of his friendship. Finally, Jerry blows a giant bubble that explodes, then whistles with all his strength. Tom, resigned, digs his grave, makes his will, leaving all his possessions to charity, and climbs into his grave. But Spike—once again —has been taken away by the pound.

Tom dashes off in pursuit of Jerry, who whistles in vain.

Note
• **Musical score: "I'm Sitting on Top of the World" (Henderson), "Darktown Strutters' Ball" (Brooks), "Spreadin' Rhythm Around" (McHugh), "You're a Sweetheart" (McHugh).**

Note
• **Musical score: "Running Wild" (Gibbs).**

1944

MOUSE TROUBLE

Directors: William Hanna,
Joseph Barbera
Producer: Fred Quimby
(Metro-Goldwyn-Mayer)
Animation: Ray Patterson, Irven
Spence, Kenneth Muse, Pete Burness
Music: Scott Bradley
Technicolor (7 min. 21 sec.)

Tom receives a copy of *How to Trap a Mouse*—a book published by Random Mouse. As he tries to apply the advice given in the book, Jerry takes to his heels. Tom sets a mousetrap. Jerry grabs the cheese, jumps on the trap, and Tom is caught in it.

Tom invents a contraption for catching Jerry with a cord tied around a tree, but once again it is Tom who gets caught. Tom then tries to arouse Jerry's curiosity. He pretends to be looking at something in his paw, but Jerry pushes Tom's fist into his own eye. Finally, Tom gets Jerry into a corner, and thinks he has him where he wants him. But Jerry screams into a stethoscope that Tom is using, and Tom's skull comes loose. Tom tries to shoot Jerry, but ends up shooting himself. Tom sets a trap, but sits down on it himself. Jerry hits Tom with a mallet. Tom brings a package and gets into it. Jerry, like a fakir, pierces the package with needles, then begins sawing away at it. Tom, wounded, is now bandaged up. He decides to use a mechanical mouse, but swallows it instead of Jerry.

Tom tears up the useless book and piles up explosives near Jerry's house. Explosion. Tom is blown up into the sky, with the mechanical mouse who keeps repeating, "Come up and see me some time."

Notes

- Musical score: "All God's Chillun Got Rhythm" (Kaper–Jurmann), "Lord and Lady Gate" (Raye–De Paul).
- This film received the Oscar for the best cartoon of 1944.
- The film was originally titled "Cat Nipped" and "Kitty Foiled."
- Some shots from this film are reused in "Jerry's Diary" (1949).
- The film describes Tom's physical decline with rare realism: He loses his hair, has to wear a wig, then loses his teeth.

1945

THE MOUSE COMES TO DINNER

Directors: William Hanna,
Joseph Barbera
Producer: Fred Quimby
(Metro-Goldwyn-Mayer)
Animation: Irven Spence, Kenneth
Muse, Pete Burness, Ray Patterson
Music: Scott Bradley
Technicolor (7 min. 18 sec.)

The black maid sets a wonderful meal on the table, full of different dishes. Jerry immediately begins to stuff himself. Tom clobbers him on the head and invites his kitten girlfriend to the table. Jerry acts as a waiter, bringing in the dishes. Tom punishes Jerry for having spit soup in his face by heating him in a spoon. Tom, in a moment of absent-mindedness, eats his own tail in a sandwich. He uses Jerry as a corkscrew.

Tom comes on strong to the kitten, who hits him over the head with a hammer that she has taken out of her purse and that is labeled "wolf pacifier." Tom lights a match under Jerry's tail. Jerry throws a pie in his face, starting a pie-throwing fight. Jerry bites Tom's tail, puts a piece of glass through it, and lights Tom's tail as though it were a candle. Tom sits down on a hot plate, which he has mistaken for a bucket full of ice cubes. He smells something burning.

"What's cookin'?" he asks the kitten, who answers, "You are, stupid." Tom, now aware of what's happening, hits the ceiling. Jerry and the kitten drop Tom into the punch, and the poor cat, baptized "S.S. Drip" by Jerry, sinks like a ship.

Notes

- Musical score: "Screwy Truant" (Bradley), "I Got It Bad" (Ellington), "You Were Meant for Me" (Brown), "Little Jerry Mouse" (Bradley), "Sweet and Lovely" (Arnheim), "Don't Get Around Much Anymore" (Ellington), "Anchors Aweigh" (Zimmerman).

- The film's original title was "Mouse to Dinner."

- Some sequences are reused in "Smitten Kitten" (1952).

MOUSE IN MANHATTAN

Directors: William Hanna,
Joseph Barbera
Producer: Fred Quimby
(Metro-Goldwyn-Mayer)
Animation: Kenneth Muse
Music: Scott Bradley
Technicolor (8 min. 6 sec.)

Notes

• Musical score: "Manhattan Serenade" (Alter), "Broadway Rhythm" (Brown).

• The film's original title was "Manhattan Serenade."

Tom and Jerry live in the country. Jerry decides to leave for town and writes a letter to Tom, who's asleep, explaining that he's leaving life in the sticks for Broadway.

Jerry arrives at Grand Central. He gets stuck in some chewing gum and sprains his neck looking up at the skyscrapers. While admiring his reflection in a lady's patent-leather-shod toe, he falls into a sewer. He climbs out through a hole and barely escapes the threat of especially heavy street traffic. He finds himself in an elevator, then in a nightclub, and finally on its terrace. He climbs up a candle to get a view of the surroundings and soon finds himself suspended from the candle over the void.

Jerry dances with some little figures on the table, but is shot into the air by a champagne bottle, which has become a real cannon. Jerry falls into a puddle; he sneezes. Some cats with "hang-dog" expressions appear. Jerry, running away, breaks the window of a jewelry shop. The police, arriving, fire at him. He's pursued in the subway.

Jerry flees and finally returns home. He tears up the letter and kisses Tom, who now wakes up, unable to understand the reason for this sudden demonstration of friendship.

"Mouse in Manhattan"

1945

TEE FOR TWO

Directors: William Hanna,
Joseph Barbera
Producer: Fred Quimby
(Metro-Goldwyn-Mayer)
Animation: Ray Patterson, Irven
Spence, Pete Burness, Kenneth Muse
Music: Scott Bradley
Technicolor (7 min.)

Tom is awkwardly playing golf and tearing up the course. Jerry pops out of a hole. Tom hits him over the head with a ball, and uses him as a tee. Tom goes on playing, but one of the balls ricochets, hitting him in the teeth. Stuck in a tree, he literally loses his head just as an avalanche of balls springs out of a tree like coins in a jackpot and buries him entirely. Jerry replaces one of the golf balls with a woodpecker egg. Tom hits the egg into the air, causing a little woodpecker to appear. He immediately attacks Tom like an airplane. Tom is propelled through the air with a golf ball Jerry has attached to him. After a ball explodes in his face, Tom is chased by a swarm of bees. Jerry chases after him, too, with a pair of clippers. He catches up with him and shaves him like a poodle. Tom takes shelter at the bottom of a lake, but Jerry points out his position to the swarm. The bees go at Tom, infiltrating the reed that Tom has used to breathe under water. Tom screams. The cat flees into the distance, and Jerry knocks him out by throwing a golf ball at him.

Notes

- Musical score: "Hoe Down" (Edens), "Shorter Than Me" (De Paul), "Spreadin' the Rhythm Around" (McHugh), "All God's Chillun Got Rhythm" (Kaper–Jurmann).

- Extracts from this film are reused in "Jerry's Diary" (1949).

FLIRTY BIRDY

QUIET PLEASE!

Directors: William Hanna,
Joseph Barbera
Producer: Fred Quimby
(Metro-Goldwyn-Mayer)
Animation: Irven Spence, Kenneth
Muse, Ray Patterson
Music: Scott Bradley
Technicolor (7 min. 13 sec.)

Directors: William Hanna,
Joseph Barbera
Producer: Fred Quimby
(Metro-Goldwyn-Mayer)
Animation: Kenneth Muse, Ray
Patterson, Irven Spence, Ed Barge
Music: Scott Bradley
Technicolor (7 min. 43 sec.)

Tom catches Jerry and prepares to eat him in a sandwich, but an eagle appears and grabs the sandwich and Jerry. Tom and the eagle tackle each other and Tom wins.

Jerry escapes from the sandwich, returns, and strikes at the eagle. Tom then appears disguised as a female eagle. The eagle is all excited, and Tom takes advantage of this to get Jerry back. Tom gets rid of the eagle, but the bird returns. Tom nails him to the ground. Jerry throws Tom to the ground. Tom gets hold of Jerry again and "kisses" the eagle with a suction cup.

The eagle offers Jerry to Tom in the form of a ring. Jerry ties Tom up and gives the rope to the eagle. Tom lands in the eagle's nest, hatching his eggs and knitting.

Notes

• **Musical score: "St. Louis Blues" (Handy), "You're a Sweetheart" (McHugh), "My Blue Heaven" (Donaldson).**

• **The film was originally titled "Love Boids."**

Tom is chasing Jerry. He fires a rifle at him. The noise awakens a sleeping dog who orders Tom to let him take a quiet nap, otherwise he'll go mad. "No more noise," orders the dog. Jerry takes this opportunity to strike at Tom, who doesn't cry out. Jerry draws a rifle on him, and Tom puts his fingers in the barrel to stifle the noise. Jerry drops a clock on the floor, but Tom plugs the dog's ears. Jerry drops some light bulbs. Tom catches them and gets an electric shock. Tom slides on some roller skates, but rocks the dog, singing to him, so as to avoid a fatal reawakening.

Tom gives the dog something to drink. At last he'll have some peace. Jerry pounds on a big drum without managing to awaken the dog. Jerry writes his will. He leaves a pie to Tom, who immediately gets it full in the face.

Jerry continues to try waking the dog. He pricks him, then slips a stick of dynamite under him, which explodes. The dog is furious.

The film ends with Tom wounded, rocking the dog's cradle, with Jerry inside.

Notes

• **Musical score: "I'm Sorry I Made You Cry" (Clesi).**

• **This film won the Oscar for the best animated film of 1945.**

SPRINGTIME FOR THOMAS

Directors: William Hanna,
Joseph Barbera
Producer: Fred Quimby
(Metro-Goldwyn-Mayer)
Animation: Ed Barge, Michael Lah,
Kenneth Muse, Irven Spence (not
credited)
Music: Scott Bradley
Technicolor (7 min. 37 sec.)

It's a perfect spring day. Jerry discovers that Tom is enamored of a young white kitten. He can think of nothing else, and he's so happy that he even gives Jerry a kiss.

The white kitten, who's reading *Har-Puss Bazaar,* drops her handkerchief and blows a kiss to Tom, who is soon struck by Cupid himself. A little green devil, who looks like Jerry, appears and urges Jerry on, explaining that this will be the end of a long friendship. Tom, utterly transformed, behaves like his girlfriend's loving pet.

Jerry now writes a perfumed letter to Dream Boy, the tomcat, inviting him to tea, and signs the note "Toodles," which is the white kitten's name. Dream Boy arrives and Tom, taking him for Toodles, kisses him by mistake. Dream Boy throws Tom into a nearby pool and begins singing for the white kitten. Tom throws him into the water, but Dream Boy, using a mallet, sends Tom, like a croquet ball, flying through one hoop after another.

Jerry still helped by his little green devil, bites Dream Boy and Tom hits him with a statue. A chase begins. Tom, sent flying into the distance, catches up with Jerry. Together they knock things around, like friends, as before. Suddenly Jerry notices a little brown mouse. Monopolized by his new flame, Jerry dismisses unhappy Tom.

Note

• Musical score: "Here Comes the Sun" (Woods), "Lovely Lady" (McHugh), "Over the Rainbow" (Arlen–Harburg), "Darktown Strutters' Ball" (Brooks), "Sweet and Lovely" (Arnheim), "Honey" (Gillespie).

THE MILKY WAIF

Directors: William Hanna,
Joseph Barbera
Producer: Fred Quimby
(Metro-Goldwyn-Mayer)
Animation: Michael Lah, Kenneth Muse, Ed Barge
Music: Scott Bradley
Technicolor (7 min. 58 sec.)

Jerry, asleep in bed, dreams he's being chased by Tom. It's a nightmare. On his doorstep he finds a nutshell and in it a little gray mouse, Nibbles, with a message that say's he's always hungry. The greedy Nibbles tries to drink Tom's milk, but Jerry stops him. Nibbles awakens Tom by catching on to his whiskers while lapping up his milk. Tom swallows Nibbles. Jerry steps in and retrieves Nibbles, preventing Tom from sucking him up through a straw. Nibbles hits Tom, who has grabbed hold of Jerry, with a hammer. Jerry and Nibbles try to escape from Tom by disguising themselves with shoe polish. Tom discovers the hoax. Nibbles accidently knocks out Jerry instead of Tom. Tom captures Jerry and chases after Nibbles. Firing a gun at Nibbles, he wounds his own tail. Tom hits Nibbles with a flyswatter. Jerry gets out of the battle in which Tom has imprisoned him. He swells up in size, roars, and frightens Tom to death. He then forces Tom to feed himself.

Notes

• Musical score: "I'll See You In My Dreams" (Jones), "I'm Nobody's Baby" (Davis).

• This film marks the first appearance of Nibbles.

1946

TRAP HAPPY

Directors: William Hanna,
Joseph Barbera
Producer: Fred Quimby
(Metro-Goldwyn-Mayer)
Animation: Kenneth Muse, Ed Barge,
Michael Lah
Music: Scott Bradley
Technicolor (7 min. 8 sec.)

Tom is chasing Jerry, but all his attempts to catch him end in failure. So he dials WA 5973, and, imitating his mistress's voice, asks the "Ajax Exterminatin' Company" to send him an "exterminator."

The exterminator, a black cat, arrives. He washes his hands in the fish bowl, paints a metal bolt to make it look like a piece of Swiss cheese, and, once Jerry has swallowed it, easily catches him with a magnet. But instead of cutting Jerry up into pieces, the exterminator slices up Tom's tail, while the mouse scampers away. Tom and the exterminator pump some poison gas into Jerry's mousehole, but he puts on a mask so that it doesn't bother him. The two cats tear up the house, and Tom knocks the exterminator out, instead of Jerry. Tom and the exterminator get a bomb, but together with Jerry, the cats toss it to one another and to Jerry, and the bomb goes off on the exterminator's head.

The cats try aiming a gun at Jerry, but only succeed in shooting themselves. They demolish the house wall. The black cat, now enraged, writes "Cat Exterminator" on his bag and fires a gun at Tom as he goes chasing after him.

1946

SOLID SERENADE

Directors: William Hanna,
Joseph Barbera
Producer: Fred Quimby
(Metro-Goldwyn-Mayer)
Animation: Ed Barge, Michael Lah,
Kenneth Muse
Music: Scott Bradley
Technicolor (7 min. 21 sec.)

Tom is attracted to a beautiful white kitten, but a watchdog named Killer (Spike) stands in the way. He knocks out the dog, ties him up, and sings to his ladylove, accompanying himself on his cello, playing it like a guitar.

The sound awakens Jerry, who gets out of bed and is hit on the head by a flower pot. Annoyed, he responds by hitting Tom with a pie containing an electric iron. Tom chases after him. Jerry jumps into the sink and pulls out the plug. Tom follows and collapses into the pile of dishes. After that, he gets caught in a window. Killer, set free by Jerry, chases Tom. In order to appear even more terrifying, he has changed his set of teeth for a more threatening one. Tom knocks out Killer, who's soon revived by Jerry. Killer threatens Tom, who makes him run after a board, which is sent bounding into the distance. Killer catches on to the trick and returns. Tom kisses the white kitten and, by mistake, Killer, who's taken her place. Talking to Killer in a Charles Boyer voice Tom discovers the truth and bashes him. He chases Jerry as far as Killer's corner.

Jerry comes out and Killer beats up Tom, who makes out his last will and testament. The film ends with Jerry playing the cello for the white kitten, with Tom's whiskers serving as the strings.

Notes

- Musical score: "Milkman, Keep These Bottles Quiet" (Raye–De Paul), "Is You Is or Is You Ain't My Baby?" (Austin–Jordan), "You Were Meant for Me" (Brown–Fain).

- Some sequences of this film were reused in "Jerry's diary" (1949), "Smitten Kitten" (1952), and "Smarty Cat" (1955).

- Tom, mistakenly thinking he's talking to his ladylove (when it's actually Killer, the watchdog), murmurs, in his Charles Boyer voice: "Ah, I love you. Ah, you set my soul on fire. It is not just a little spark, it is a flame, a big roaring flame. Ah, I can feel it now."

1947

CAT FISHIN'

PART TIME PAL

Directors: William Hanna,
Joseph Barbera
Producer: Fred Quimby
(Metro-Goldwyn-Mayer)
Animation: Kenneth Muse, Ed Barge,
Michael Lah
Music: Scott Bradley
Technicolor (7 min. 54 sec.)

Directors: William Hanna,
Joseph Barbera
Producer: Fred Quimby
(Metro-Goldwyn-Mayer)
Animation: Michael Lah, Kenneth
Muse, Ed Barge
Music: Scott Bradley
Technicolor (7 min. 50 sec.)

Tom is planning a fishing trip, despite the many signs that forbid it and the presence of Spike, the formidable watchdog. Spike bites Tom's paw. Tom begins fishing anyway, using Jerry as bait. Jerry finds the water too cold. The fish begin to laugh, but Jerry strikes out at them. Suddenly a shark appears. Jerry escapes. Tom disguises Jerry as a worm, and once again the mouse has to make his escape from the shark. Tom, swinging an oar, hits Jerry, not the man-eating fish. The shark bites Tom's tail, which, thanks to Jerry, looks like bait. The shark wakes up Spike. Tom jumps into the water, then pulls Spike in. But Jerry hitches Tom's line onto Spike and Spike they fishes Tom out.

Spike chases Tom, who is fished out by Jerry and still threatened by the angry dog.

Tom is warned by the black maid: Either he protects the refrigerator from Jerry's raiding or he'll be put out of the house! So Tom carefully guards the refrigerator, but he falls into a barrel of cider while trying. Now drunk, he empties the refrigerator himself. The turkey squeezes him. He dives into a cake, but the maid arrives, and Jerry, in a moment of generosity, hides Tom.

Tom wants to kick the maid in the rear, but Jerry stops him. Tom wants to set her on fire, but Jerry puts a stop to this, too. He chases after Jerry, but accidentally swallows the contents of a bottle labeled "Bay Rum." He gets drunk again.

Tom is set on pouring a pitcher of water on the maid, who is now asleep. He succeeds and the maid chases after him. The house is soon completely torn up.

Outside, in the dark of night, the maid continues to chase after Tom.

Notes
- Musical score: "Milkman, Keep These Bottles Quiet" (Raye–De Paul).
- The film was initially to be titled "Fair Weathered Friend."

Notes
- Musical score: "Trolley Song" (Martin–Blane).
- Some of the film's shots were reused in "Life with Tom" (1953) and in "Smarty Cat" (1955).

1 9 4 7

THE CAT CONCERTO

Directors: William Hanna,
Joseph Barbera
Producer: Fred Quimby
(Metro-Goldwyn-Mayer)
Animation: Kenneth Muse, Ed Barge,
Irven Spence
Music: Scott Bradley
Technicolor (7 min. 49 sec.)

Tom, a virtuoso pianist, enters the concert hall to the applause of the audience. He adjusts the height of his seat, wipes his paws, begins to play, checks his collar, lifts his coat tails and, finally, begins Liszt's Hungarian Rhapsody no. 2. Jerry, asleep inside the piano, is suddenly awakened and set into motion by the hammers.

He takes revenge by beating the measure out of time. Tom strikes a key under which Jerry is standing, and Jerry strikes another. Tom hits him with a key. Jerry shuts the piano lid on Tom, crushing his paws. He comes out with a pair of scissors to cut off Tom's toes and, having removed a few keys, replaces them with a mousetrap. Tom catches Jerry and locks him into the piano stool. Jerry raises it, then lets it drop sharply. Tom shuts him up in the hammers, which strike Jerry and send him reeling. Completely groggy, Jerry has had enough. He begins to play with the hammers. Tom knocks himself out trying to catch up with the keys and finishes, exhausted. Jerry, wearing "tails" is applauded in triumph!

Notes

• Musical score: "Credits" (Chopin; arr. Scott Bradley), "The Cat's Concerto" (Liszt; arr. Scott Bradley), "On the Atchison, Topeka, and the Santa Fe" (Warren–Mercer).

• This film won the Oscar for the best cartoon of the year.

• Tom is well portrayed, with an air of superiority, complacent, "inspired," and condescending to his applauding public.

• Of particular note is the smooth passage from the Hungarian Rhapsody no. 2 to the song, "On the Atchison, Topeka, and the Santa Fe," sung by Judy Garland, Ray Bolger, and chorus in *The Harvey Girls* (1946), directed by George Sidney.

72

DR. JEKYLL AND MR. MOUSE

Directors: William Hanna,
Joseph Barbera
Producer: Fred Quimby
(Metro-Goldwyn-Mayer)
Animation: Ed Barge, Michael Lah,
Kenneth Muse, Al Grandmain
Music: Scott Bradley
Technicolor (7 min. 24 sec.)

Jerry is resolved to drink the milk that Tom has just prepared for himself. Hidden inside a trunk, he slurps the milk with the aid of a straw. Tom hides the milk in a safe, but Jerry appears again.

Tom now prepares a diabolical mixture, one so potent that it dissolves the spoon. A fly takes a bit, screams in pain, and dies on the spot. Jerry drinks it all up and begins to grow larger. Tom grows frightened as Jerry comes toward him.

Tom hides in the safe. Jerry takes him out, hits him, and becomes a little mouse once again. He drinks some more of the brew, begins to swell up again, and once again shrinks back to his original size. He burns Tom's tail in the waffle iron, then pushes him into the refrigerator. Jerry makes some more of the diabolical mixture. Tom gets out of the refrigerator and drinks it. He swells to a huge size, then shrinks way down. Jerry starts after him, armed with a fly swatter.

Note
• The film was nominated for the Academy Award for the best cartoon of 1947.

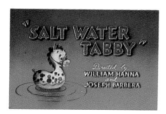

SALT WATER TABBY

Directors: William Hanna,
Joseph Barbera
Producer: Fred Quimby
(Metro-Goldwyn-Mayer)
Animation: Ed Barge, Michael Lah,
Kenneth Muse
Music: Scott Bradley
Technicolor (7 min. 16 sec.)

The setting is a beach. Tom jumps into the water and dives into garbage. He then meets a white kitten and eats her hotdog. Jerry, hidden in the picnic basket, devours the food. Jerry bites Tom, and while chasing after Jerry, Tom is bitten by a crab. Jerry corners Tom by closing the beach umbrella. The crab reappears and pinches Tom again. Tom breaks his teeth on an "oyster" sandwich from Jerry. Tom pours salt instead of sugar into his coffee. With his mouth now on fire, he swallows water to ease the burning and spits it out on the white kitten. He buries himself in the sand while looking for Jerry. Jerry shuts Tom up in the umbrella again but is then caught in a bottle and shaken up by Tom. Jerry is then sent flying into the air but shortly afterward Tom, who has now swallowed a buoy, is sent flying too. Jerry sails off on the picnic basket, converted into a boat.

Notes

• Musical score: "Here's to the Girls" (Edens).

• Certain sequences are reused in "Smitten Kitten" (1952).

• Tom's behavior toward the white kitten is noticeably crude: He eats her hotdog and spits water at her.

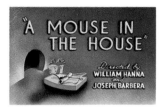

1 9 4 7

A MOUSE IN THE HOUSE

Directors: William Hanna,
Joseph Barbera
Producer: Fred Quimby
(Metro-Goldwyn-Mayer)
Animation: Kenneth Muse, Ed Barge,
Richard Bickenbach, Don Patterson
Music: Scott Bradley
Technicolor (7 min. 49 sec.)

The black maid is upset to discover that Jerry and the two house cats (Tom and another feline) have wreaked havoc in the refrigerator. Furious, she threatens the two cats, telling them that from now on there's room for only one. Only the cat who can catch Jerry will be allowed to remain in the house!

The two cats set about looking for Jerry, helped for the time being by Jerry himself. They go after him, but he strikes them with a log. Tom draws a pistol on the other cat, but a small creature comes out of his weapon. The cats corner Jerry in the oven, but he escapes by striking a match and causing the oven to explode in their faces. Having finally managed to catch Jerry, they fight over who owns him. Like boxers, they rest for a moment, while Jerry, like a fight manager, "advises" each of them. The fight resumes, and Jerry surrenders to the second cat, but Tom gets him back. He dresses up like the black maid and knocks out the other cat. The latter then disguises himself as the maid as well, and knocks Tom out. When the maid appears, the cats hit her on her behind, each one mistaking her for the other cat.

The maid, furious, puts both cats out. And Jerry, too, has to leave.

Note

- Musical score: Reuse of the music from "Part Time Pal" (Bradley).

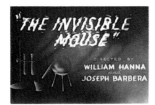

THE INVISIBLE MOUSE

Directors: William Hanna,
Joseph Barbera
Producer: Fred Quimby
(Metro-Goldwyn-Mayer)
Animation: Ed Barge, Richard
Bickenbach, Don Patterson, Irven
Spence
Music: Scott Bradley
Technicolor (8 min. 42 sec.)

Tom lures Jerry with a piece of Swiss cheese, but soon has his paw hit by an iron and his head by a cuckoo clock. Jerry breaks a plate over Tom's head. Then Jerry falls into a bottle of invisible ink, and becomes invisible himself. The mouse eats the cheese. Tom again has his paw hit by an iron. Jerry gives Tom an electric shock, takes his milk bowl, empties it in one gulp, and spits the milk back in his face. He then places matches between Tom's toes and sets them on fire.

But Tom catches sight of Jerry's shadow as the mouse eats a banana. He spreads flour on the ground and traces Jerry's footsteps. The mouse twists his muzzle.

Tom grabs the mouse and hits him with a book, but Jerry escapes and hits back with a golf club.

Jerry strikes Spike the dog, who holds Tom responsible for this attack and chases after him. Jerry becomes visible again as he continues to drink Tom's milk.

Note

• **Musical score: "Here's to the Girls" (Edens).**

KITTY FOILED

Directors: William Hanna,
Joseph Barbera
Producer: Fred Quimby
(Metro-Goldwyn-Mayer)
Animation: Irven Spence, Kenneth
Muse, Irving Levine, Ed Barge
Music: Scott Bradley
Technicolor (7 min. 20 sec.)

Tom chases after Jerry while a canary looks on. Tom threatens Jerry. The canary intervenes and bashes Tom, who lands in the canary's cage, under lock and key. Jerry catches Tom's tail in the window blind. Jerry and the canary hide out in Jerry's home. The canary tries to reenter his cage, but Tom, intercepting, swallows him. Jerry catches Tom's tail in a floor slat and ends by escaping, disguised as a redskin, with the newly escaped canary disguised as a papoose. Tom sees that he's been tricked and chases after them. The canary traps him in a bearskin and threatens him with a pistol. Jerry then lets a light bulb fall to the floor. Tom, hearing the noise, thinks it's gunfire. He thinks he's been fatally wounded, imagines he's already dead, and falls to the ground. Jerry and the canary congratulate each other on their success, but Tom reappears. He gets Jerry and ties him to the railway tracks. He then bears down on him, driving a train. The canary throws a bomb shaped like a bowling ball and the ground suddenly opens up before the train, and Tom is swallowed by the yawning hole.

Jerry and the canary, now rid of Tom, swing back and forth inside the canary cage, humming "My Blue Heaven."

Notes

• Musical score: "Here's to the Girls" (Edens), "My Blue Heaven" (Donaldson).

• Some shots of this film were reused in "Life with Tom" (1953).

• Of particular interest is the moment when Tom, believing himself desperately wounded, already sees himself buried and juggles desperately with a coin, parodying George Raft's performance in Howard Hawks' *Scarface* (1932).

THE TRUCE HURTS

Directors: William Hanna,
Joseph Barbera
Producer: Fred Quimby
(Metro-Goldwyn-Mayer)
Animation: Kenneth Muse, Ed Barge,
Ray Patterson, Irven Spence
Music: Scott Bradley
Technicolor (8 min. 59 sec.)

Tom, Jerry, and Butch (Spike) chase and fight each other. They end by signing a nonaggression pact, proposed by Butch. From then on, everything goes well. They sleep together and share the morning milk. Along comes a black cat who catches Jerry. Tom appears and saves Jerry. The black cat is disgusted. A dog catches sight of Tom, attacks him, and gets ready to eat him. Butch appears and saves Tom.

The three new friends take a walk in the street. Along the way, they are splattered by a passing meat truck. A big steak falls out of the delivery van. The sharing process poses a number of problems, since each of the three has a definite idea of the share (the largest one) he wants.

Soon Butch and Tom are fighting and Jerry steals the entire piece of meat. The three former friends fight it out; the steak disappears, carried off by a stream of water into the gutter. Butch, furious, tears up the nonaggression pact, and Tom, Jerry, and Butch begin to fight again.

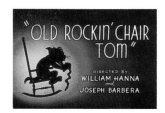

1948

OLD ROCKIN' CHAIR TOM

Directors: William Hanna,
Joseph Barbera
Producer: Fred Quimby
(Metro-Goldwyn-Mayer)
Animation: Fred Barge, Ray Patterson,
Irven Spence, Kenneth Muse
Music: Scott Bradley
Technicolor (7 min. 39 sec.)

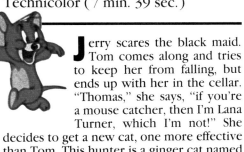

Note

- Musical score: "Happy Days Are Here Again" (Ager), "Running Wild" (Gibbs), "Sleepy Head" (Donaldson), "Sing Before Breakfast" (Brown), "Over the Rainbow" (Arlen), "Worry Song" (Fain), "We're Off to See the Wizard" (Arlen).

Jerry scares the black maid. Tom comes along and tries to keep her from falling, but ends up with her in the cellar. "Thomas," she says, "if you're a mouse catcher, then I'm Lana Turner, which I'm not!" She decides to get a new cat, one more effective than Tom. This hunter is a ginger cat named Lightnin'. Lightnin' swings into action. He throws Jerry out, keeps him from reentering the house, and makes fun of Tom, whom he considers too old and out of date. He uses the situation to empty the refrigerator and has Tom accused of his thefts. The maid is furious with Tom and has Lightnin' chase him out of the house. Tom and Jerry, suddenly united, make Lightnin' swallow an iron and then, with a strong magnet, they manipulate him as they wish. The magnet prevents Lightnin' from intervening when the maid is threatened by Jerry. Tom is then able to "happen along" and "save" the maid. Tom puts Lightnin' out of the house and hurts his foot with the iron that had been swallowed by the ginger cat. The maid apologizes for her behavior and nurses the wounded Tom.

Note

- Musical score: "Spreadin' Rhythm Around" (McHugh), "Trolley Song" (Martin–Blane), "I'm Sitting on Top of the World" (Henderson).

PROFESSOR TOM

Directors: William Hanna,
Joseph Barbera
Producer: Fred Quimby
(Metro-Goldwyn-Mayer)
Animation: Ray Patterson, Irven
Spence, Kenneth Muse, Ed Barge
Music: Scott Bradley
Technicolor (7 min. 47 sec.)

Tom is teaching a sleepy young cat the basics of mouse hunting. Jerry arrives and scratches the chalk across the blackboard. Tom forces the unwilling young cat to set out on the chase after Jerry. The cat breaks through the wall of the shower and takes a bath. Tom goes after Jerry, but Jerry teaches the cat peaceful coexistence. Instead of knocking Jerry out with a vase, the

cat gives it to Jerry, and the mouse uses it to strike Tom.

Tom tries to smoke out Jerry, who has taken refuge in his hole, but when he blows cigar smoke in Jerry's direction, it's Tom who gets sick. The young cat finally catches Jerry, but refuses to surrender him to Tom. Tom gives the cat a spanking. Jerry breaks Tom's tail off and Tom, trying to put Jerry out of the house, finds himself on the other side of the door. Jerry bars his reentrance, and Tom gets shut up in the mailbox. The young cat hits him with a bat and leaves with Jerry, his new-found friend, to the tune of "We're Off to See the Wizard."

Note
• Musical score: "We're Off to See the Wizard" (Arlen).

MOUSE CLEANING

Directors: William Hanna,
Joseph Barbera
Producer: Fred Quimby
(Metro-Goldwyn-Mayer)
Animation: Ray Patterson, Irven
Spence, Kenneth Muse, Ed Barge
Music: Scott Bradley
Technicolor (7 min. 47 sec.)

The black maid is cleaning the house, which is now spic and span and in perfect order. Tom and Jerry come in from outside, chasing after each other. Tom dirties up everything in his way. The maid makes him clean up and tells him: "If I find one grain of dust when I come back, there's going to be one cat less here." She goes off to market. Jerry throws ashes on the floor. Tom immediately picks them up. Tom throws a tomato at Jerry, but the tomato splatters against the wall; Jerry pours ink into Tom's bucket, so that he stains the wall while trying to clean it.

Jerry juggles with some eggs and a pie. Tom manages to get the eggs back into their carton, but the pie hits him in the face. Jerry has an old, broken-down horse carried into the house, and Tom throws it out. Exhausted, Tom falls asleep and Jerry spreads ink on the paws of his old enemy. Tom starts chasing after Jerry and dirties up the entire

house with his inky paws. Tom throws Jerry down into the cellar and cleans up, but Jerry has arranged for the coal order to be delivered in the parlor, not in the cellar, as planned!

The maid, who has returned, is carried off by the flood of coal. She asks Tom, whose head has turned black, if her cat is around. Tom answers negatively, in a drawl, but the maid catches sight of the rest of the cat's body, which has remained gray. She understands what has happened and bombards him with pieces of coal. Tom dodges the first few, but is eventually hit and knocked out by the coal.

Note
• According to Mark Kausler, Kenneth Muse was responsible for the animation in the sequence in which Tom juggles with the eggs and the ink pad. Ed Barge was in charge of the animation of the old nag and the coal, while Ray Patterson and Irven Spence did the last sequences.

POLKA-DOT PUSS

Directors: William Hanna,
Joseph Barbera
Producer: Fred Quimby
(Metro-Goldwyn-Mayer)
Animation: Kenneth Muse, Ed Barge,
Ray Patterson, Irven Spence
Music: Scott Bradley
Technicolor (7 min. 2 sec.)

Tom is playing with Jerry, using him as a yo-yo. The black maid wants to put him out for the night, but the weather is terrible. Tom fakes a sneeze. The maid allows him to lie down by the fire. Tom gets his nose caught in the trap meant for Jerry. He falls asleep and before he wakes up, Jerry paints red dots all over his face. Jerry shows him an article that says that the whole country is suffering an epidemic of measles. Jerry listens to Tom's heartbeat through a stethoscope and when Tom begins to listen, the mouse puts the stethoscope up against the alarm clock, which suddenly goes off. Jerry strikes Tom's knee with a hammer and nurses him in his own fashion. He covers him with ice cubes and puts him in the refrigerator, then takes him out, completely frozen, and deposits him in the oven, then under a cold shower. Tom, discovering that his red spots are all gone, figures out that he's been tricked. Furious, he grabs a sword and catches up with Jerry who really does have measles. He takes preventive measures, but falls ill as well.

The Little Orphan
DIRECTED BY
WILLIAM HANNA
AND
JOSEPH BARBERA
ACADEMY AWARD WINNER OF 1948

1 9 4 9

THE LITTLE
ORPHAN

Directors: William Hanna,
Joseph Barbera
Producer: Fred Quimby
(Metro-Goldwyn-Mayer)
Animation: Irven Spence, Kenneth
Muse, Ed Barge, Ray Patterson
Music: Scott Bradley
Technicolor (7 min. 50 sec.)

Jerry is reading *Good Mousekeeping* when along comes Nibbles, the little orphan mouse Jerry invited to Thanksgiving dinner. Nibbles, as always, is hungry. He drinks Tom's milk while the cat is fast asleep. The black maid places a stuffed chicken on the festively decorated table. Nibbles climbs up on the table with the help of a noodle, which he swallows once he's on the table. He devours a pie, a candle, and, upon eating a whole orange, takes on a round shape. Jerry returns Nibbles to his normal shape, but the orange, flung into the air, is swallowed by Tom. He swings into action and, disguised as an Indian, attacks. Jerry fires a bottle of champagne at him. Nibbles attacks Tom, who goes after Jerry, who sticks Tom with a fork. Tom changes his target and catches Nibbles, but is knocked out by Jerry.

Tom shoots flaming arrows—actually dried flowers—then attacks with a knife, catching Jerry. Nibbles counterattacks. Tom is flung out of the house by Nibbles, with a champagne bottle. Exhausted, Tom gives up. But Nibbles attacks the dishes and devours them all before Tom and Jerry even get a chance to taste them.

Notes

- **Musical score: "Throw Another Log on the Fire" (Tobias–Scholl–Mencher).**
- **This film received the Oscar for the best cartoon in 1949.**
- **Some shots from this film are reused in "Life with Tom" (1953).**
- **This film was remade in CinemaScope as "Feedin' the Kiddie" (1957).**

1949

HATCH UP YOUR TROUBLES

Directors: William Hanna,
Joseph Barbera
Producer: Fred Quimby
(Metro-Goldwyn-Mayer)
Animation: Ed Barge, Ray Patterson,
Irven Spence, Kenneth Muse
Music: Scott Bradley
Technicolor (7 min. 50 sec.)

An egg falls out of a woodpecker's nest and rolls over to Jerry's home. Soon a baby woodpecker comes out of the egg. He immediately starts devouring everything in sight made of wood. Jerry puts him outside, back into the nest, but the baby bird follows him around, mistaking him for his mama. Jerry discovers the chick is still around and with his eyes popping out of his head, puts him outside again and chases him away.

Tom is reading the *Saturday Evening Puss,* when he discovers the presence of the little woodpecker. He goes after him, while the chick calls for his mama. Jerry comes rushing in and saves him. The chick goes after everything made of wood, but he's eaten by Tom. The baby woodpecker continues his damage inside Tom, who is soon covered with holes. Tom drinks some water, which starts coming out of the holes. The baby woodpecker manages to emerge by boring a hole in Tom's teeth. Tom tries to hit Jerry with a little axe, but he's continually prevented by the little woodpecker, who pecks away energetically at his skull, causing the sound of a pneumatic drill. Tom stops up the bird's beak with a cork so that he can't get at him.

Tom chases after Jerry with his axe, but the little woodpecker has become free. He makes a clever sketch, starts working on a pole, which then falls on Tom, who gets buried beneath the ground.

The mother woodpecker arrives and retrieves her child, and the baby woodpecker kisses a smiling Jerry.

Notes

- Musical score: "M-O-T-H-E-R" (Morse).
- Remade in 1956, under the title "The Egg and Jerry."
- This film was nominated for an Academy Award.

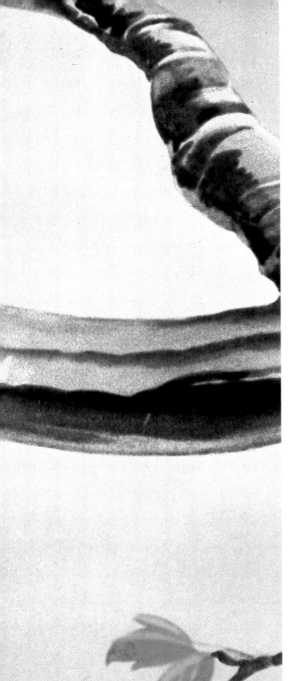

HEAVENLY PUSS

Directors: William Hanna,
Joseph Barbera
Producer: Fred Quimby
(Metro-Goldwyn-Mayer)
Animation: Ray Patterson, Irvin
Spence, Kenneth Muse, Ed Barge
Music: Scott Bradley
Technicolor (7 min. 48 sec.)

Tom is chasing after Jerry. He tears the carpet up from the staircase, but is crushed under a piano. He ascends to heaven, where he discovers a line of cats waiting for the Heavenly Express. He finds Butch, who's been killed by a dog; Frankie, fatally wounded by an iron while singing; Aloysius, who's been run over; and Fluff, Puff, and Muff, three little kittens who have been drowned.

Tom is told that in order to be admitted to paradise, he must absolutely obtain Jerry's signature on a certificate of forgiveness. Otherwise, he'll go to hell, where a sneering devil awaits him. Tom has only one hour in which to get the certificate signed.

Tom gets to work. He offers a cake to Jerry. But Jerry, instead of signing the certificate, throws the fountain pen's ink at him. Tom tries imitating Jerry's signature, but a voice sternly reminds him of his duty. Jerry tears up the certificate and the devil immediately calls out for Tom. Tom explains the situation to Jerry, imitating the devil, as he does so. Jerry agrees to sign the certificate. But Tom is swallowed up in the ground, and falls into a caldron.

Tom suddenly wakes up. He's been lying near the fire and is awakened by a burning coal. It's all been a horrible nightmare! Tom kisses Jerry, who can't understand this sudden affection.

Notes

• Some sequences from this film are used again in "Shutter Bugged Cat" (1967).

• The given name of Spence, the animator, is spelled Irven or Irvin, depending on the film in question. We have reproduced the spelling as it appears on each credit list.

THE CAT AND THE MERMOUSE

Directors: William Hanna,
Joseph Barbera
Producer: Fred Quimby
(Metro-Goldwyn-Mayer)
Animation: Kenneth Muse, Ed Barge,
Ray Patterson, Irvin Spence,
Al Grandmain
Music: Scott Bradley
Technicolor (7 min. 49 Sec.)

Tom is relaxing on the beach. Jerry is fishing, but it's Tom who suddenly appears in the water. Tom sinks into the water, all the way to the bottom of the sea. He sees fish passing by. He begins swimming behind a big turtle, and discovers a mouse-siren: Jerry. He chases him and swallows him. Jerry gets out through Tom's ear. Tom sees a row of seahorses going by, with Jerry behind them. He catches him with a lasso. But then Tom is hit on the head by an anchor. Jerry is chased by a swordfish. Tom knocks him out and tries somewhat awkwardly to shove the wounded fish's jaw back into place. The swordfish stabs Tom and starts to chase after him, but runs into a mast, and Tom blocks his way completely. No sooner has he got rid of the swordfish than he finds himself confronting a threatening octopus. Jerry tries to rescue him from the arms of the octopus.

Jerry saves Tom by artificial respiration, making him cough up the water he's swallowed.

Note

• Musical score: "Here's to the Girls" (Edens), "Horses" (Gay).

LOVE THAT PUP

Directors: William Hanna,
Joseph Barbera
Producer: Fred Quimby
(Metro-Goldwyn-Mayer)
Animation: Ed Barge, Ray Patterson,
Irven Spence, Kenneth Muse
Music: Scott Bradley
Technicolor (7 min. 55 sec.)

Butch the dog is relaxing quietly with his son Pup by his side. He feeds him affectionately. But Tom is chasing Jerry and, after being hit with a rake and a shovel, catches Pup instead of Jerry. Butch is furious and threatens Tom. Jerry comes out from behind Pup's ear, but Tom arrives and Jerry hides in Butch's mouth. Tom tears Butch's teeth out and plays with them, like castanets. He returns them and carries off Pup, mistaking him again for Jerry.

Pup runs away, and Tom takes his place, being petted by Butch, who treats him like his own son, until he discovers the truth.

Tom takes off, but is hit full in the face with the rake. He manages to lure Butch away with a big steak and locks him in a shed. He corners Jerry under a barrel. But Jerry runs away, and Butch appears, mad with rage. Butch discovers his son under the barrel and attacks Tom, who makes a dash for the exit.

It is night time again. Tom is outside. Jerry relaxes quietly, between Butch and Pup.

Notes

• Remade in 1957, under the title "Tops with Pops."

• Extracts from this film were reused in "Matinee Mouse" (1966).

• This marks the first appearance of Butch and Pup, his darling son, the future Spike and Tyke.

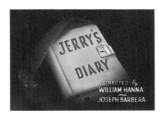

1 9 4 9

JERRY'S DIARY

Directors: William Hanna,
Joseph Barbera
Producer: Fred Quimby
(Metro-Goldwyn-Mayer)
Animation: Kenneth Muse, Ed Barge
Music: Scott Bradley
Technicolor (9 min. 43 sec.)

Tom is placing traps around Jerry's mouse hole, but he hears Uncle Dudley on the radio announcing a be-kind-to-animals week. He removes all the traps and replaces them with gifts. But he discovers that Jerry isn't there. He finds Jerry's diary and reads it.

April 5. Tom plays golf and uses Jerry as a tee. Tom strikes a ball that ricochets, returning with brute force to break his teeth (from "Tee for Two," 1945).

May 12. Tom is reading and laughing. Jerry, now curious, comes out of his hole. Tom shuts him up inside the closed book. Jerry pretends to be looking at something in his hands. Tom is curious, and Jerry strikes him in the eye (from "Mouse Trouble," 1944).

June 3. Tom chases Jerry and lands in the sink, from which Jerry has drained the water. Tom is caught in a window, with his tongue hanging out of his mouth (from "Solid Serenade," 1946).

July 4. Tom tries to wipe Jerry out with a stick of dynamite. Both Tom and Jerry try to get rid of it, but keep passing it to each other. The stick finally explodes in Tom's face. A second stick of dynamite also explodes in his face (from "The Yankee Doodle Mouse," 1943).

Tom, infuriated by the reminder of these various misadventures, begins to disperse the gifts intended for Jerry, and when the mouse appears he throws a pastry at him. Jerry, astonished, can't understand why.

Notes

- Musical score: "Shorter Than Me" (de Paul).

- The ending of this film is used once again in "Matinee Mouse" (1966).

1 9 4 9

TENNIS CHUMPS

Directors: William Hanna,
Joseph Barbera
Producer: Fred Quimby
(Metro-Goldwyn-Mayer)
Animation: Ray Patterson, Irvin
Spence, Ed Barge, Kenneth Muse
Music: Scott Bradley
Technicolor (6 min. 49 sec.)

Tom and a black, cigar-smoking cat are about to play a championship tennis match. Jerry brings Tom the necessary rackets and balls. Tom soon becomes the victim of a number of "accidents": His racket catches on fire, he swallows three balls coming from his opponent, and he gets caught in the net.

Jerry, with a wink in Tom's direction, gives him a bomb that looks like a tennis ball. Tom serves it, and the black cat explodes. Jerry then gives the black cat a hard object that looks like a tennis ball. The black cat serves this one. It hits Tom, who, under its impact, breaks up into pieces. The two cats go at Jerry, who has swallowed a ball. Jerry does a tightrope walk on the net, and

the two cats end up playing against the mouse. They pursue him, but he pelts them with balls from the court's machine. The cats find themselves suspended together from a tree like marionettes, both prisoners of the net, while Jerry, the winner, takes the championship trophy.

Note

• **Musical score: "All God's Chillun Got Rhythm" (Kaper–Jurmann).**

1950

LITTLE QUACKER

Directors: William Hanna,
Joseph Barbera
Producer: Fred Quimby
(Metro-Goldwyn-Mayer)
Animation: Irven Spence, Ray
Patterson, Ed Barge, Kenneth Muse
Music: Scott Bradley
Technicolor (7 min. 7 sec.)

A duck lays an egg. Tom steals it, intending to cook it. A duckling hatches out of the egg, so Tom looks up a recipe for roast duck. The duckling runs away, and hides in Jerry's bed.

Tom cuts his own tail with the chopper he's been holding, the roof falls on his head,

a falling tree buries him in the ground, and he still can't catch Jerry and the duckling.

He tries a decoy, and the duckling, thinking he hears his mother, rushes in. Jerry appears and replaces the decoy with a stick of dynamite that explodes in Tom's face. Tom recovers, tries to catch up with his opponents, and is hit by the hammer with which he vainly tried to attack Jerry and the duckling. Tom chases after Jerry and the duckling with a pair of clippers and, on his way, attacks the mama duck. She calls for help from her husband Henry. The duck shaves Tom with the clippers. Finally, we see Jerry relaxing in a little rubber boat, drawn by the duck, with the duckling sitting beside Jerry.

Notes

- **Musical score: "Love That Pup" (Bradley).**

- **This film marks the first appearance of the duckling, who is included in seven more films.**

SATURDAY EVENING PUSS

Directors: William Hanna,
Joseph Barbera
Producer: Fred Quimby
(Metro-Goldwyn-Mayer)
Animation: Ed Barge, Kenneth Muse,
Irvin Spence, Ray Patterson
Music: Scott Bradley
Technicolor (6 min. 18 sec.)

The black maid is making herself up before going out for the evening. Tom takes this chance to invite three of his friends over to the house: a black, a ginger, and a beige cat. The four cats play music and drink to their hearts' content. Jerry, awakened by the music, is unable to sleep. He tells Tom that he's fed up and the cats begin to go after him. He breaks the record player, closes the piano lid, and goes back to his hole. Tom turns the record player back on. Jerry comes out again and takes the record player away. Tom ties Jerry up and the three cats continue with their music and noise.

Jerry manages to telephone the maid, who has been playing bridge at the Lucky Seven Saturday Night Bridge Club. She arrives in a fury and throws out the four cats, who form a totem pole and put some hot music on the radio. Jerry is furious!

Notes

- Musical score: "Darktown Strutters' Ball" (Brooks).
- The film's original title was "Party Cat."

TEXAS TOM

Directors: William Hanna,
Joseph Barbera
Producer: Fred Quimby
(Metro-Goldwyn-Mayer)
Animation: Kenneth Muse, Ray
Patterson, Irvin Spence, Ed Barge
Music: Scott Bradley
Technicolor (6 min. 34 sec.)

The setting is "Dude Ranch." Tom, dressed as a cowboy, is practicing with a lasso and trying to catch Jerry. The arrival of an attractive white kitten immediately transforms him into a veritable bull. He rolls a cigarette (which Jerry moistens), writes "Howdy" with its smoke, and strums a guitar, pretending to sing, while Jerry plays a record of "If You're Ever Down in Texas Look Me Up." Jerry plays the record at high speed, then at low speed. Tom, exasperated, clobbers him.

Jerry brands Tom with a red-hot iron. Tom, throwing his lasso, accidentally tears off the horns of a bull, who shows his displeasure. Tom puts the horns back somewhat clumsily, and the bull begins to chase him.

The bull changes his horns to appear more threatening and finds Tom hiding among the chickens. Tom hits him in the eye with an egg. The bull charges at him. Tom lights a last cigarette and is knocked out. Jerry arrives, dressed as a cowboy, kisses the white kitten and mounts Tom, who yells in pain, as he feels the spurs digging into his sides.

Notes

• Musical score: "Ventriloquist Cat" (Bradley), "I Tipped My Hat and Slowly Rode Away" (Markes–Charles), "Sweet and Lovely" (Arnheim), "If You're Ever Down in Texas, Look Me Up" (Shand–Dunham).

• Certain shots from this film are reused in "Smitten Kitten" (1952) and in "Cruise Cat" (1952).

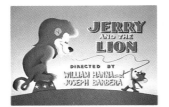

1 9 5 0

JERRY AND THE LION

Directors: William Hanna,
Joseph Barbera
Producer: Fred Quimby
(Metro-Goldwyn-Mayer)
Animation: Irvin Spence, Ed Barge,
Kenneth Muse, Ray Patterson
Music: Scott Bradley
Technicolor (7 min. 13 sec.)

Tom, who's been asleep, suddenly awakens and discovers that Jerry is emptying the refrigerator. He rushes over, but Jerry escapes. The radio announces the escape of a ferocious lion. Tom, terrified, barricades the door, dresses up in a hunting outfit, and arms himself.

Jerry discovers the lion in the cellar. He's not at all ferocious; in fact, he's quite mild. The lion explains to Jerry that he's fed up with the circus noise, its silly music, and the crackling of popcorn wrappers. He wants to go back to his native jungle. Meanwhile, he hopes to get a meal, since he hasn't eaten in days.

Tom tracks Jerry down and suddenly discovers the lion hiding behind the curtains. The lion throws Tom into the mantelpiece, like a coin into a slot machine, and Tom—as if he'd won!—gets an avalanche of bricks on his head.

Tom opens an umbrella and suddenly comes up against the lion, who was hidden inside it. Tom closes the door by passing his hand around the door's other side, but gets knocked out by the lion. Tom then gets chased by Jerry and flies out of the house.

Jerry finally has some peace and quiet. He puts the lion on board the launch of the S.S. Africa. The boat leaves, and Jerry, alone on the quay, wipes away a few tears.

Notes

- Musical score: "Love That Pup" (Bradley), "Sleepy Time Gal" (Whiting), "Blaze Away" (Holzman).
- The film's original title was "Hold That Lion."

SAFETY SECOND

Directors: William Hanna,
Joseph Barbera
Producer: Fred Quimby
(Metro-Goldwyn-Mayer)
Animation: Ray Patterson, Ed Barge,
Kenneth Muse, Irvin Spence, Al
Grandmain
Music: Scott Bradley
Technicolor (7 min. 7 sec.)

Jerry and Nibbles have just awakened. It's the Fourth of July. Nibbles brings in a pile of fireworks, but Jerry is nervous around explosives. A firecracker goes off in his face. Jerry puts Nibbles in the corner, but the tiny mouse produces another tiny firecracker, which again blows up in Jerry's face.

Jerry is relaxing. Tom puts a firecracker under his hammock and grabs hold of him. Jerry pretends to be inspecting something in his hand. Tom's curiosity is piqued, and Jerry catches him off guard and hits him. Tom begins chasing Jerry, who hides out in a hole. Tom goes at the hole with a pickax, until he's blown away by a rocket lighted by Nibbles. Nibbles hides inside a firecracker and sends the terrified Tom running off. Tom discovers what's really happening, begins to laugh at the tiny firecracker, which goes off, with enormous strength, right in his face!

Tom, enraged, tries to blow everything up, but blows himself up instead. He is sent flying into space with a rocket that explodes in a spectacular fireworks display. When a firecracker goes off in Jerry's face again, Nibbles, who's responsible for it all, promises Jerry he'll be good.

Notes

* **Musical score: "Love That Pup" (Bradley), "Here Comes the Sun" (Woods–Freed).**
* **The film was originally titled "F'r Safety Sake."**

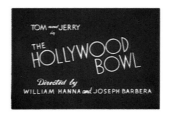

TOM AND JERRY IN THE HOLLYWOOD BOWL

Directors: William Hanna,
Joseph Barbera
Producer: Fred Quimby
(Metro-Goldwyn-Mayer)
Animation: Kenneth Muse, Irven
Spence, Ray Patterson, Ed Barge
Music: Scott Bradley
Technicolor (7 min. 22 sec.)

The setting is the Hollywood Bowl. Tom, the orchestra's conductor, arrives on stage. The orchestra is composed entirely of cats who look like Tom. The orchestra launches into "Die Fledermaus" by Johann Strauss. Jerry emerges from his mouse hole, which resembles a miniature Hollywood Bowl, and he, too, conducts the music.

Tom is leading the orchestra. He throws Jerry out, but he returns. Tom and Jerry dance to the music. Jerry throws out Tom, who of course returns. Tom whirls Jerry around, then throws him way out. Jerry returns. Tom keeps him away, using his baton like a billiard cue, but Jerry takes his revenge by breaking the baton. Jerry then puts Tom on skates and sends him rolling away into the distance. Tom gets run over by a bus. Now Jerry can finally direct the orchestra, but Tom reappears. He tears up Jerry's tail coat and flattens him between the cymbals. Jerry gets back at him by sawing the floor away around each musician, so that all the members of the orchestra disappear, one by one. Only Tom, now a one-man orchestra, remains. Jerry bows to the audience, while Tom, exhausted, sinks into the ground.

Notes

* **Musical score: "Die Fledermaus" (Overture; Johann Strauss).**
* **The orchestra, composed entirely of Tom's "look-alikes," recalls that of "An American in Paris" (1951), directed by Vincente Minnelli, in which all the musicians performing Gershwin's Concerto in F were played by Oscar Levant.**

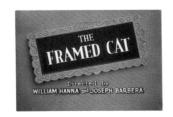

THE FRAMED CAT

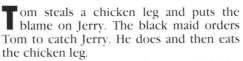

Directors: William Hanna,
Joseph Barbera
Producer: Fred Quimby
(Metro-Goldwyn-Mayer)
Animation: Ed Barge, Kenneth Muse,
Irven Spence, Ray Patterson
Music: Scott Bradley
Technicolor (7 min. 11 sec.)

Tom steals a chicken leg and puts the blame on Jerry. The black maid orders Tom to catch Jerry. He does and then eats the chicken leg.

Jerry wants revenge. He sees Butch the dog with a bone, steals it, and plants it on Tom. Butch discovers that his bone is gone (his tongue, transformed into a hand, gropes for it and can't find it) and he gets angry with Tom. Butch buries his bone, but Jerry swipes it and ties it to Tom's tail. Butch chases Tom and takes back his bone, but Jerry sticks a vise into the bone and places a magnet in Tom's mouth, so that he attracts the bone.

Butch rushes at him, but the bone, when grabbed, always returns to Tom. Finally, we see Tom running away from the bone, which is drawn to the magnet; Butch bent on retrieving his bone; and Jerry ensconced in a tin can.

Notes

- Musical score: "Love That Pup" (Bradley), "Sing Before Breakfast" (Brown–Freed).

- For the film's 1957 rerelease, the black maid was replaced with a white servant.

95

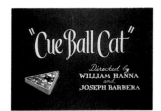

CUEBALL CAT

Directors: William Hanna,
Joseph Barbera
Producer: Fred Quimby
(Metro-Goldwyn-Mayer)
Animation: Kenneth Muse, Irvin
Spence, Ed Barge, Ray Patterson
Music: Scott Bradley
Technicolor (7 min. 2 sec.)

The scene is a poolroom. Tom starts shooting pool and wakes Jerry up by hitting him with the number 10 ball. Jerry comes out of his hole and runs away. Tom forces him to come back by shooting a ball in his direction. He uses Jerry as a ball and makes him jump through a flaming triangle. Jerry swings into action and throws balls at Tom, using a cue stick as a baseball bat. Tom falls into a bottle while trying to catch a ball as in baseball. He then attaches the fire hose to the cue stick and tries to get Jerry. Tom sends two cue sticks flying toward him. Jerry hits him in the mouth with the rake. Jerry is pursued by a series of balls, which Tom finally has to swallow. Tom stabs himself in the back while trying to get Jerry with a cue stick. Jerry starts to shoot pool and sends the yellow ball—the number 1—flying at Tom, who swallows it.

Note

• **Musical score: "Love That Pup" (Bradley), "Winning Fight" (Holzmann).**

CASANOVA CAT

Directors: William Hanna,
Joseph Barbera
Producer: Fred Quimby
(Metro-Goldwyn-Mayer)
Animation: Irvin Spence, Ray
Patterson, Ed Barge, Kenneth Muse
Music: Scott Bradley
Technicolor (7 min. 4 sec.)

Tom, all dressed up, is leading Jerry, who is tied up in ribbons. He's going to call on Toodles, the white kitten, who has just inherited a million dollars. Tom offers a gift to Toodles. It is Jerry, whom he has wound up like a music box. Tom makes Jerry, disguised as a black mouse, dance on a plate heated by the flame of a match. Jerry takes revenge by squeezing Tom's tail in an ashtray. Jerry sees Butch, the black cat, singing "Over the Rainbow" in the street. He sends him the newspaper article announcing Toodles' inheritance, and Butch immediately rushes over to Toodles' apartment and kisses her. He throws Tom in the goldfish bowl. But Tom sends Butch flying out through the air until only his smile (briefly) remains. Butch comes back and buries Tom in the couch, with a weight in his mouth.

The two cats chase each other. Jerry kisses Toodles, and ties the two cats together. He then leaves in a car with Toodles, whom he covers with passionate kisses.

Notes

• Musical score: "Love That Pup" (Bradley), "Broadway Rhythm" (Brown–Freed), "Lovely Lady" (McHugh–Koehler), "Three Letters in the Mail Box" (Jurmann–Webster), "Over the Rainbow" (Arlen–Harburg), "You Were Meant for Me" (Brown–Freed).

• When Butch, the black cat, disappears, he leaves his smile, cigar, and eyes. This is reminiscent of Lewis Carroll's Cheshire Cat.

JERRY AND THE GOLDFISH

Directors: William Hanna,
Joseph Barbera
Producer: Fred Quimby
(Metro-Goldwyn-Mayer)
Animation: Irvin Spence, Ray
Patterson, Ed Barge, Kenneth Muse
Music: Scott Bradley
Technicolor (7 min. 21 sec.)

Jerry gives a cracker to his friend, Goldy the fish. But Tom, listening to the radio, hears the new recipe by "François, the great chef." He's intrigued and, needing a fish to cook, grabs Goldy. Jerry intervenes, striking Tom and putting Goldy back into a glass of water. Jerry takes off with Goldy, and they both pass right through Tom's head.

Jerry tries to put Goldy back into his bowl, but Tom tries to fry him in a pan. Once again, Jerry rescues Goldy and knocks Tom out. Tom sets off after them, and is knocked into the shape of first an accordion and then a sausage. Tom fires a revolver, breaks the cup in which Goldy is hiding, grabs him, and puts him on the grill. Jerry comes back and grabs Goldy, but Tom drops him into the toaster. Jerry puts Tom's tail into the clothes mangle, but Tom gets hold of Goldy and cooks him in the pot. Jerry substitutes a stick of dynamite for a carrot Tom has prepared, and the cat soon puts his tail, not Goldy, into the pot. He runs off with the pot and ends up in the sky, watching the earth disappear in the distance.

Jerry, now that Tom is gone, does a bit of underwater swimming with Goldy.

Note
- Musical score: "Love That Pup" (Bradley).

JERRY'S COUSIN

Directors: William Hanna,
Joseph Barbera
Producer: Fred Quimby
(Metro-Goldwyn-Mayer)
Animation: Ray Patterson, Ed Barge,
Kenneth Muse, Irvin Spence
Music: Scott Bradley
Technicolor (6 min. 39 sec.)

The scene is Hogan's Alley, full of cats, knocked out and done in. They are the victims of Muscles Mouse, Jerry's indestructible cousin. Jerry writes to Muscles Mouse, asking him for help in his battle against Tom. Muscles Mouse arrives just as Tom is throwing sticks of dynamite into Jerry's hole. Muscles begins by placing one in Tom's mouth. It goes off. Muscles Mouse threatens Tom. Tom goes into training in order to withstand his new opponent, but Muscles Mouse blows up his fist like a balloon and knocks Tom out. Muscles Mouse is then knocked down into the cellar by a bowling ball Tom has dropped on him. Muscles reappears and throws the ball at Tom, who then breaks into several Toms shaped like bowling pins.

Tom calls out a "cleaning" firm, "Dirty Work, Inc." Three alley cats, whom we've already seen tossing coins into the air, appear. Muscles Mouse knocks them all out. Tom, now desperate, becomes servile. Muscles Mouse gives his suit to Jerry and leaves.

Jerry, disguised as Muscles Mouse, strikes terror into Tom, who slavishly licks his paws.

Notes
- Musical score: "Lydia, the Tattoed Lady" (Arlen–Harburg), "The Dickey Bird Song" (Fain–Dietz).
- The film's previous titles were "City Cousin" and "Muscles Mouse."
- This film was nominated for the Academy Award as the best animated film of its year.

1951

SLEEPY-TIME TOM

Directors: William Hanna,
Joseph Barbera
Producer: Fred Quimby
(Metro-Goldwyn-Mayer)
Animation: Ed Barge, Kenneth Muse,
Irvin Spence, Ray Patterson
Music: Scott Bradley
Technicolor (7 min. 5 sec.)

Tom and three pals are returning from a night on the town, drinking. They're singing as they go. Tom reaches home. The black maid scolds him and tells him he should be chasing Jerry instead of going to sleep.

Jerry, however, arranges things so that Tom, exhausted by his night of debauchery, can collapse—which of course brings a scolding from the maid. Tom runs after Jerry, then falls asleep again. He's hit on the head with a baseball bat while waiting for Jerry, who puts a cushion under his head.

Tom is fed up. He drinks a few quarts of coffee and swells up to a huge size. He tries in vain to keep his heavy eyelids open. Finally, he paints eyes on his lids so as to sleep in peace.

Encouraged by some screens arranged by Jerry, Tom goes to bed. The maid throws him outside. Tom falls asleep with his head pillowed on a brick, but his three drinking pals arrive and carry him off for another night on the town.

Note
- Musical score: "Love That Pup" (Bradley), "Sleepy Time Gal" (Whiting), "Sleepy Head" (Donaldson–Kahn).

HIS MOUSE FRIDAY

Directors: William Hanna,
Joseph Barbera
Producer: Fred Quimby
(Metro-Goldwyn-Mayer)
Animation: Kenneth Muse, Irvin
Spence, Ray Patterson, Ed Barge
Music: Scott Bradley
Technicolor (7 min. 11 sec.)

Note
- **Musical score: "Chloe" (Moret).**

Tom is shipwrecked, all alone, in the middle of the ocean. Starvation has reduced him to eating his shoe. Finally, he spies an island. He swims to the island and is hit on the head by a coconut. He can't manage to break it open. He sees a tortoise and breaks his teeth on the animal's shell. Then he notices Jerry, dressed as Robinson Crusoe. He wants to make a meal of him, but Jerry knocks him out. The chase begins. Tom finds himself in a native village, apparently deserted. Jerry is playing a drum, making Tom feel suddenly anxious. Jerry disguises himself as a native cannibal mouse. He has Tom prepare a giant caldron, with himself as the main course. Tom, who's sitting in the soup, tastes it, salts it, but soon discovers that the mouse who had frightened him so is none other than Jerry, who's just lost his grass skirt.

Tom is suddenly surrounded by a band of black cannibal warriors. He takes to his heels. So does Jerry. They scamper off together.

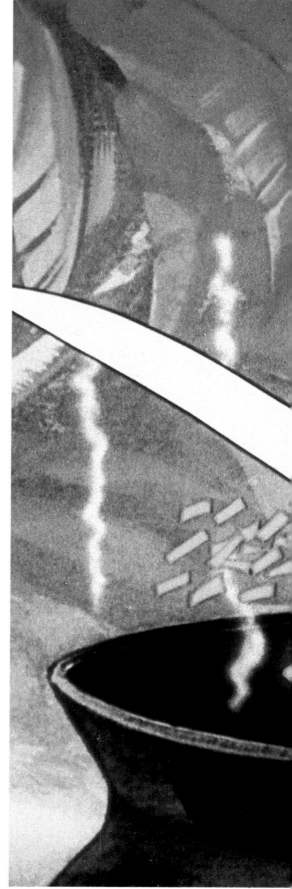

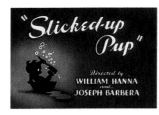

1951

SLICKED-UP PUP

Directors: William Hanna,
Joseph Barbera
Producer: Fred Quimby
(Metro-Goldwyn-Mayer)
Animation: Ed Barge, Kenneth Muse,
Irven Spence, Ray Patterson
Music: Scott Bradley
Technicolor (6 min. 19 sec.)

Butch is bathing his son Pup in a big tub. "That's my boy," he says, proudly, "nice and clean." But Tom is chasing Jerry and causes Pup to fall into the mud. Butch, furious, forces Tom to clean Pup up and warns him what will happen should he find Pup dirty again. Tom tries to prevent Pup from getting dirty. He cleans him up when the dog gets slighty spattered with mud. Jerry writes on Pup's back. Tom cleans him off. Jerry throws a tomato, and Tom dodges it, but seeing that it's headed toward Pup, he sacrifices himself and willingly takes it full in the face. Pup is accidentally showered with ink. Tom paints him over, but Jerry mixes up the pots and Pup becomes multicolored. Tom wants to wash Pup, but instead he mistakenly covers him with tar. Butch arrives and Tom has Pup pass for a little black rooster. But Pup bites Tom's tail. Tom throws Pup in the washing machine. And now Butch goes into action. He throws Tom into the machine and turns it on. Tom, locked inside, is shaken up as Butch, Pup, and Jerry watch, laughing.

Note

• Musical score: "Love That Pup" (Bradley), "The Dickey Bird Song" (Fain–Dietz).

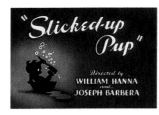

1951

NIT-WITTY KITTY

Directors: William Hanna,
Joseph Barbera
Producer: Fred Quimby
(Metro-Goldwyn-Mayer)
Animation: Ray Patterson, Ed Barge,
Kenneth Muse, Irven Spence
Music: Scott Bradley
Technicolor (6 min. 33 sec.)

The maid, exasperated at Tom's disorder, hits him with a broom, and the cat begins to behave like a mouse. He gives Jerry a piece of Swiss cheese and a kiss. He settles into Jerry's hole, lies down on the bed, and it collapses under him. The maid, utterly at a loss, telephones for the doctor. Jerry is fed up with all this; he reads an article in a medical encyclopedia that says that Tom will return to normal if he receives another blow on the head. Jerry then sets up an ingenious system that will propel Tom up to the ceiling and turn him into a cat again, but Tom is hit in the head by the bowling ball that catapulted him up and instead remains a mouse. Tom manages to avoid being hit by a piano, an iron, and an anvil, but after a series of surprises, he's hit on the head—accidentally—by an ironing board and turns back into a cat.

The maid, who's also bent on curing him, strikes him with a baseball bat. Immediately, Tom turns into a mouse, and Jerry, disgusted, sees Tom returning to his mousehole to kiss him.

Note

• Musical score: "Love That Pup" (Bradley).

CAT NAPPING

Directors: William Hanna,
Joseph Barbera
Producer: Fred Quimby
(Metro-Goldwyn-Mayer)
Animation: Irven Spence, Ray
Patterson, Ed Barge, Kenneth Muse
Music: Scott Bradley
Technicolor (6 min. 52 sec.)

Jerry is resting peacefully in a hammock. Tom arrives, wants to use it, and makes Jerry slide into a puddle. Tom settles in the hammock, but Jerry returns, makes him fall out, and takes his place. Tom sends Jerry flying into the air. Tom, back in the hammock, sees an ant colony arriving. He gets them to carry Jerry away, but the mouse sends them on a detour, and the hammock suddenly rolls up as they pass. Jerry drops a frog into Tom's glass; he swallows it and begins jumping around. Jerry attacks Tom with a pair of clippers, reducing him to a string of paper dolls, and catapults him into the air. Tom passes a plane, then a bird, and goes into a dive, breaking into pieces as he plunges into a pond.

Butch the dog (Spike) settles into the hammock next. Tom, who has returned, knocks him out and discovers—too late—that he's mistaken the dog for Jerry.

As the film ends, Butch is making Tom fan Jerry, who's lying next to the dog in the hammock.

Note

• Musical score: "Love That Pup" (Bradley), "Here Comes the Sun" (Wood–Freed), "Man on the Flying Trapeze" (Lea–Leybourne).

1952

THE FLYING CAT

Directors: William Hanna,
Joseph Barbera
Producer: Fred Quimby
(Metro-Goldwyn-Mayer)
Animation: Kenneth Muse, Irven
Spence, Ed Barge, Ray Patterson
Music: Scott Bradley
Technicolor (6 min. 44 sec.)

Tom steals the cage that houses the canary. Jerry comes along, trips Tom, and the cage goes flying into a tree. The canary flies away and Tom, who was chasing Jerry, stops running. He's knocked out by a falling pole. Jerry and the canary hide together in the canary's house. Tom goes looking for them. Dragged down by a heavy weight, he falls to the ground. He climbs a ladder, which the canary sets on fire. Tom tries reaching his opponents with a swing, a perch, and, finally, by dressing like a bat and trying to fly, but he ends up stuck in the mailbox. Nevertheless, Tom does manage to fly in his bat costume. Jerry sees this and warns the canary, who remains skeptical. Tom chases after the canary but is caught on the roof of the house. It has been turned inside out by Jerry and the canary and is covered with nails. Tom captures Jerry, but the canary snatches his bat costume away, and he falls to the ground, splitting a tree in the process. The canary takes Jerry away. Tom goes after them, but is stopped by a train in a tunnel and reduced to a railway traffic signal. Jerry and the canary celebrate their victory in the back of the train.

Notes
- Musical score: "Love That Pup" (Bradley).
- Some of the sequences are used again in "Matinee Mouse" (1966).

THE DUCK DOCTOR

Directors: William Hanna,
Joseph Barbera
Producer: Fred Quimby
(Metro-Goldwyn-Mayer)
Animation: Irven Spence, Ray
Patterson, Ed Barge, Kenneth Muse
Music: Scott Bradley
Technicolor (7 min. 3 sec.)

Tom aims a gun at a flock of ducks and hits them. A duckling is wounded and falls to the ground. Jerry hides him. The duckling has a broken wing. He tells Jerry what has happened. Jerry makes a splint for him, but the duckling wants to rejoin his friends. Tom goes after them, and Jerry makes Tom's gun go off in the cat's face. Tom uses a decoy to attract the duckling. He aims at him and hits an enormous pig, who flattens him out. Jerry, who is fed up, ties the duckling to a huge anvil, so he can't get away. But Tom uses another decoy. The duckling flattens Tom with his anvil by hitting him on the head with it, then flies away *with* the anvil! Tom takes aim and cuts the cord that ties the duckling to the anvil. Tom realizes the full extent of his action too late. He digs his grave, smokes a last cigarette and dies, crushed by the anvil.

The duckling goes back to his friends and flies away with them. Jerry says good-bye with a decoy.

Note
- Musical score: "Love That Pup" (Bradley).

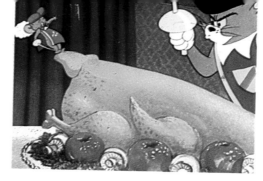

1952

THE TWO MOUSEKETEERS

Directors: William Hanna,
Joseph Barbera
Producer: Fred Quimby
(Metro-Goldwyn-Mayer)
Animation: Ed Barge, Kenneth Muse,
Irven Spence
Music: Scott Bradley
Technicolor (7 min. 21 sec.)

T om, one of the cardinal's guards, is assigned to stand watch over the table prepared for a banquet. Should he fail in his
duty, he will be guillotined. But Jerry and
Nibbles, two of the king's musketeers, arrive
on the scene. They open a bottle of champagne, which attracts Tom's attention. Tom
sees Nibbles making a sandwich. He attacks,
and Nibbles flees. He captures the mouse,
but Jerry arrives and attacks him in turn.
Tom and Jerry fight a duel. Nibbles steps in
and scalps Tom's back with a halberd, but
falls into a wine glass. Now slightly tipsy,
Nibbles provokes Tom, who has been preparing to roast some meat. Jerry comes
along and again fights a duel with him.
Meanwhile, Nibbles stuffs a small cannon
with food, then fires. Jerry and Nibbles leave
with the food, as Tom is decapitated. "Poor,
poor Pussycat," says Nibbles.

Notes

• **Musical score: "Soldiers of Fortune" (Romberg–
Kahn).**

• **This film won the Oscar of that year for the best cartoon.**

• **This is the first film in which Tom plays a cardinal's
guard, and Jerry and Nibbles two of the king's musketeers. The film includes several lines in French spoken
by Nibbles.**

1952

SMITTEN KITTEN

Directors: William Hanna,
Joseph Barbera
Producer: Fred Quimby
(Metro-Goldwyn-Mayer)
Animation: Kenneth Muse
Music: Scott Bradley
Technicolor (7 min. 49 sec.)

J erry has just been cutting up Tom's tail
into a string of paper dolls. Tom is furious
and wants to kill him, but just then he spies
a young gray kitten and gets excited. A little
green devil appears and warns Jerry: "Every
time Tom meets a kitten, he falls in love, and
that means you have problems again."

He reminds Jerry of a past episode. Tom
was on the beach with a white kitten, eating
her hot dog, when he got hit on the head by
a banana and discovered that Jerry was stealing food from the picnic basket. He reacted
quickly and threw Jerry into the water (excerpt from "Salt Water Tabby," 1947). The
little green devil continues his warning with
another episode: Tom hit Jerry, who was
eating. He called up his ladyfriend and invited her to dinner. Jerry, on top of the
table, was forced to serve the dishes. He
blew on the soup to cool it off. Tom heated
the spoon in which Jerry was sitting, and he
fell into the butter (taken from "The Mouse
Comes to Dinner," 1945).

The little devil recalls still another adventure to Jerry: Tom, a cowboy, fell under the
spell of a young cowgirl kitten. Intending to
seduce her, he rolled a cigarette and made
Jerry moisten the paper. He lit the cigarette
while drawing his revolver, and wrote the
word "Howdy" in the air with its smoke.
Tom is flirting with the kitten at poolside.
The little green devil tells one last story:
Tom was playing the cello at the foot of his
ladylove's balcony, singing "Is You Is or Is
You Ain't My Baby?" Jerry was awakened by

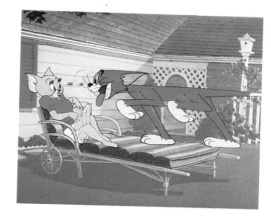

the noise and was hit over the head by a flower pot (sequence from "Solid Serenade," 1946).

The little devil gives Jerry a needle, but Jerry suddenly gets excited at the sight of a mouse. The devil's disgusted. And just then he meets a young little girldevil, who gets him excited, too.

Note
- Musical score: "Blue Moon" (Rodgers), "Here's to the Girls" (Edens).

TRIPLET TROUBLE

Directors: William Hanna,
Joseph Barbera
Producer: Fred Quimby
(Metro-Goldwyn-Mayer)
Animation: Ray Patterson, Ed Barge,
Kenneth Muse, Irven Spence
Music: Scott Bradley
Technicolor (7 min. 9 sec.)

Tom and Jerry are at it again. The maid takes in three little cats who have been put in her charge. But these charming little cats are real terrors. They immediately start bothering Tom, who's been told to be particularly nice to the three: a ginger, a tan, and a black cat. Jerry's amused by all this, but the kittens attack him, too, and begin to chase after him. They make mincemeat of him. Tom starts to laugh, but the three little cats send him flying up to the ceiling and flat back on the ground.

Tom and Jerry soon find themselves kicked out. This is the last straw.

The three kittens are busy sipping milk when Jerry starts to get at them. Tom attacks with various sorts of ammunition; he throw pies and then a watermelon at them. He grabs hold of them and throws them from his flying machine.

The three little cats are now squeezed into the clothes dryer, which goes round and round, and Jerry gives them a good spanking, one after the other.

Note
- Musical score: "Love That Pup" (Bradley).

1 9 5 2

LITTLE RUNAWAY

Directors: William Hanna,
Joseph Barbera
Producer: Fred Quimby
(Metro-Goldwyn-Mayer)
Animation: Ed Barge, Kenneth Muse,
Irven Spence, Ray Patterson
Music: Scott Bradley
Technicolor (7 min. 4 sec.)

A black baby seal has escaped from the "G.H. Bros. Circus." Jerry discovers him in the pool, where he was intending to take a bath. The baby seal confesses that he's had enough of circus life. He's hungry and wants a fish. So Jerry goes to steal Tom's fish. He hides behind the fish, which suddenly looks to Tom as if it has come to life. He applauds this, but the baby seal swallows the fish and Tom gets mad. He threatens to hit Jerry, but the seal butts in and turns him on his nose like a ball. The circus offers a reward of $10,000 for the return of the baby seal. Tom captures him, but Jerry soon sets him free again. Tom, perched on a carriage train, chases the seal across telegraph wires. The seal dives into a glass of water. Tom follows and can't get out of the glass. Tom, using a tire, disguises himself as a seal. He plays ball with the baby seal, but the circus animal warden arrives and carries Tom off, thinking he is the seal.

Tom comes out into the circus ring, to the sound of applause. He's feeling pleased, and gets a fish right in his face.

Note
• Musical score: "Love That Pup" (Bradley), "Flying Feet March" (Axt).

FIT TO BE TIED

Directors: William Hanna,
Joseph Barbera
Producer: Fred Quimby
(Metro-Goldwyn-Mayer)
Animation: Kenneth Muse, Irven
Spence, Ray Patterson, Ed Barge
Music: Scott Bradley
Technicolor (6 min. 49 sec.)

Butch the dog has a nail stuck in his paw. Jerry comes along and takes it out. Butch, in gratitude, gives Jerry a little bell and tells him, "When you're in danger, ring the bell." Tom appears, takes the bell and rings it. Butch arrives, swings into action and knocks Tom out.

Tom is taking care of Jerry and feeding him; he's afraid of the bell and its consequences. But there's an announcement in the newspaper saying that all dogs are to be tied up. Tom no longer has anything to fear. He provokes Butch, who's tied up, and beats him up. Jerry, threatened by Tom, rings several bells, but to no avail. Butch doesn't come to his rescue. Tom continues to provoke Butch, but the dog manages to get his hands on Tom, and the cat, stripped of his skin, suddenly appears in red underwear.

Tom has a good time ringing the bell. He runs no risk at all. But the law is repealed.

Jerry strikes Tom. Butch comes along and knocks him out. Butch proudly strolls along with Tom on a leash, while Jerry rings the famous bell.

Notes

• Musical score: "Love That Pup" (Bradley).

• Some shots of this film are reused in "Smarty Cat" (1955).

PUSH-BUTTON KITTY

Directors: William Hanna,
Joseph Barbera
Producer: Fred Quimby
(Metro-Goldwyn-Mayer)
Animation: Irven Spence, Ed Barge,
Kenneth Muse
Music: Scott Bradley
Technicolor (6 min. 33 sec.)

The maid is cleaning the house. Jerry is strolling along quietly with a piece of cheese. Tom feels too lazy to run after him.

But the maid receives a package in the mail; it's Mechano, "the cat of tomorrow," a robot-cat. Tom laughs at it, and so does Jerry. But the maid sets Mechano into action, and he catches Jerry and puts him out of the house. Tom, disgusted, takes his knapsack and leaves the house.

Every time Jerry tries to return, he's caught by Mechano and kicked out. Now Jerry sends in some mechanical mice. Mechano goes wild and destroys the whole house while chasing after them and he eventually breaks himself. Tom, called to the rescue, returns. He is welcomed by the maid,

but he has swallowed the Mechano's main spring. Jerry has only to flick the switch and Tom begins destroying everything in sight, while chasing a mechanical mouse.

Notes

• Musical score: "Love That Pup" (Bradley), "You Can't Do Wrong Doin' Right" (Rinker—Huddleston).

• This is the last film in which Mammy Two Shoes appears.

"Fit to Be Tied"

A-7

CRUISE CAT

Directors: William Hanna,
Joseph Barbera
Producer: Fred Quimby
(Metro-Goldwyn-Mayer)
Animation: Irven Spence, Ray
Patterson, Ed Barge, Kenneth Muse
Music: Scott Bradley
Set Design: Robert Gentle
Technicolor (7 min. 2 sec.)

The captain of the "S.S. Aloha" warns Tom that if he discovers a mouse on board, he's going to change mascots. Tom sees Jerry climbing aboard and throws him off. Jerry returns, but Tom sends him back to the quay. Another of Jerry's attempts to steal on board ends in failure, but he manages to climb up by using the anchor. Tom discovers Jerry, but slips on a bar of soap and falls into the water. Jerry jumps into the pool. Tom chases after him, but Jerry has emptied the pool, and Tom breaks into pieces. Jerry pushes Tom overboard. Tom returns, but the stick of dynamite he prepared for Jerry goes off in his face. Tom and Jerry enter the ship's auditorium. The cartoon "Texas Tom" is just beginning. They stop to look at it. In the film, Tom lassoes Jerry, and Jerry is pricked by a cactus. Tom laughs, but not Jerry. The film continues, and now it's Tom's turn to play the victim. Jerry finds this very funny. Tom, now furious, hurls him overboard, but a bird brings him back, and Tom, to his horror, discovers him in the captain's place. The captain throws Tom into the brig. From his prison, Tom sees Jerry bound for shore on a surfboard, playing a ukelele.

Notes

• **Musical score: "Hawaiian War Chant" (Noble–Leleohaku), "It's a Most Unusual Day" (McHugh–Adamson), "Makin' Love Mountain Style" (Scholl–Moulton).**

• **This film contains extracts from "Texas Tom" (1950).**

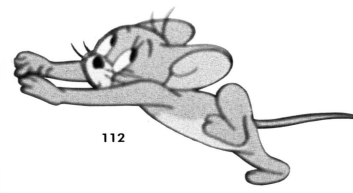

1952

THE DOG HOUSE

Directors: William Hanna,
Joseph Barbera
Producer: Fred Quimby
(Metro-Goldwyn-Mayer)
Animation: Kenneth Muse, Irven
Spence, Ray Patterson, Ed Barge
Music: Scott Bradley
Set Design: John Didrik Johnsen
Technicolor (6 min. 39 sec.)

S pike is busy building the kennel of his
dreams. Tom comes along and destroys
it while chasing Jerry. Then he hits Spike.
The dog gets angry and demands to be allowed to construct his kennel in peace. He
slams Tom against a pole, and Tom gets hit
over the head with a mailbox. Tom continues chasing Jerry. Spike gets angry again,
and strikes out at Tom, but the kennel is
accidentally crushed by Spike himself. The
chase begins again. Tom hits Spike, who falls
on top of the kennel. Tom chases after Jerry
and flattens him with a steamroller. He then
tries to blow up Jerry with a stick of dynamite, but the kennel explodes instead.

Spike repairs the kennel, but Tom cuts
down a telegraph pole, which falls on top of
him. Spike places his kennel in a tree, but
Tom cuts down the tree, and Spike and his
kennel fall to the ground. Tom catches Jerry
with his lasso, and pulling Jerry toward him,
pulls Spike and the kennel as well. Spike
whips Tom into repairing and repainting the
damaged kennel.

Note
* Musical score: "Love That Pup" (Bradley), "My Blue
Heaven" (Donaldson–Whiting).

1953

THE MISSING MOUSE

Directors: William Hanna,
Joseph Barbera
Producer: Fred Quimby
(Metro-Goldwyn-Mayer)
Animation: Ray Patterson, Ed Barge,
Kenneth Muse, Irven Spence
Music: Edward Plump
Set Design: Robert Gentle
Technicolor (6 min. 33 sec.)

J erry empties the refrigerator. Tom comes
along and stops him. He pinches his tail
in a mousetrap. A little bottle of white shoe
polish falls on Jerry, and he becomes completely white. Just then, the radio announces that an "explosive" white mouse
has escaped. Tom sees Jerry and is terrified.
He tries telephoning for help, but in vain.
He tries to keep Jerry from falling (for fear
he'll explode). He lets the piano fall on his
own head to keep it from hitting Jerry. Jerry
lets an iron fall on Tom. He hits Tom with a
hammer and frightens him by beginning to
jump, but finally falls into the sink and turns
brown again. Tom now realizes what's been
happening, and strikes Jerry with the hammer. And Jerry figures out the situation now
that he sees himself in the mirror. Tom puts
Jerry out of the house, but the real white
explosive mouse arrives. Tom starts washing him energetically and catching sight of
Jerry, realizes the situation. He ages several
decades.

The radio announces that the explosive
white mouse no longer presents any danger.
Tom attacks the white mouse. Everything
explodes! Tom, amidst the wreckage, speaks
in a voice from beyond the grave. The radio
continues to announce that the danger of
explosion is over.

Note
* The music for this film is not by Scott Bradley.

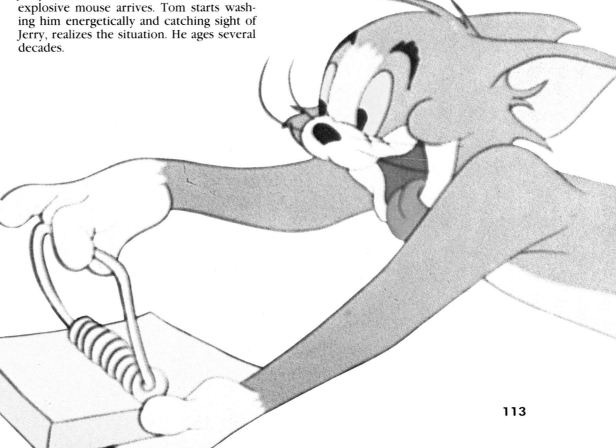

1953

JERRY AND JUMBO

Directors: William Hanna,
Joseph Barbera
Producer: Fred Quimby
(Metro-Goldwyn-Mayer)
Animation: Kenneth Muse, Irven
Spence, Ed Barge
Music: Scott Bradley
Set Design: Robert Gentle
Technicolor (7 min. 13 sec.)

A circus train roars through the night. A baby elephant falls out of the train and rolls down the hill until he lands in Tom's basket. He sucks up Tom's milk with his trunk. Tom thinks Jerry has done it and gets ready to hit him, but the little elephant arrives to suck up Jerry, and then some peanuts. The noise attracts Tom, who doesn't know what's going on.

Jerry paints the little elephant brown to make him look like a huge mouse. Tom sees Jerry and the elephant, one after the other. They both hit him. Tom sees Jerry, then the baby elephant, then both of them. He's flabbergasted.

Tom puts out a giant mousetrap in order to catch what he believes is a huge mouse, but the little elephant sucks it up with his trunk, and Tom gets caught in the trap. He is flattened out on the staircase by the little elephant. Determined to pay him back, he opens fire with a gun. But the mother elephant finally arrives. She finds her son and disguises herself as a giant mouse. Tom, terrified, suddenly finds himself facing three "mice," one of whom is a giant. He runs away screaming.

Note

- Musical score: "Love That Pup" (Bradley), "On the Atchison, Topeka, and the Santa Fe" (Warren–Mercer).

114

1953

JOHANN MOUSE

Directors: William Hanna,
Joseph Barbera
Producer: Fred Quimby
(Metro-Goldwyn-Mayer)
Animation: Kenneth Muse, Ray
Patterson, Ed Barge, Irven Spence
Music: Scott Bradley
Set Design: Robert Gentle
Piano arrangements composed and
interpreted by Jakob Gimpel
Narration: Hans Conreid
Technicolor (7 min. 57 sec.)

This is the story of Johann Mouse, who lived in Vienna, in Johann Strauss' own house.

Every day, when Johann Strauss plays the piano, Johann Mouse (Jerry) dances. Day after day, Tom tries unsuccessfully to catch him. Johann Strauss leaves on a trip and Tom knows that without music he doesn't stand a chance of catching Johann Mouse. So he learns to play the piano—in six lessons!—and quickly becomes a virtuoso pianist. Johann reappears. Tom goes after him. He plays with him and captures Johann/Jerry.

The staff of the Strauss house applauds. Tom plays the piano and Jerry dances.

The news soon spreads. Tom and Johann/Jerry are invited to the emperor's palace. Tom plays the piano and Jerry dances. But

Tom stops playing, and starts chasing Jerry. The mouse escapes and bows to the applauding audience.

Note
• **This film received the Oscar for the year's best animated film.**

1953

THAT'S MY PUP

Directors: William Hanna,
Joseph Barbera
Producer: Fred Quimby
(Metro-Goldwyn-Mayer)
Animation: Kenneth Muse, Ray
Patterson, Ed Barge, Irven Spence
Music: Scott Bradley
Set Design: Robert Gentle
Technicolor (7 min. 23 sec.)

Spike is teaching his son Tyke things he'll find useful in life: sitting up to beg from his master, burying bones in good places, and, above all, cleverness in chasing cats. At this point Tom arrives, in pursuit of Jerry. Spike scares Tom with his growling. He loses his skin in fright. Spike tells Tom he has reason to fear Tyke. Tyke barks at Tom, making Spike happy and proud. Jerry, who's threatened by Tom, makes a noise that attracts Tyke, and then Spike. Jerry barks, frightening Tom. Soon Tom sees what's really going on. He hides, but Tyke pulls him by the tail. Tom takes his revenge, putting Tyke all the way on top of a flagpole. Tyke falls, and Spike, now furious, takes his revenge. He spreads grease on the mast and chases Tom who climbs up, then redescends. So it goes with little Tyke barking away and Spike enjoying the "ferocity" of his offspring.

Note
• **Musical score: "Love That Pup" (Bradley).**

JUST DUCKY

Directors: William Hanna,
Joseph Barbera
Producer: Fred Quimby
(Metro-Goldwyn-Mayer)
Animation: Irven Spence, Ed Barge,
Ray Patterson, Kenneth Muse, Al
Grandmain
Music: Scott Bradley
Set Design: Robert Gentle
Technicolor (7 min. 57 sec.)

S ix little ducklings hatch out of their
shells. They follow their mother, but the
sixth one can't swim and almost drowns. He
calls for his mother and cries. Jerry arrives
and tries unsuccessfully to teach him to
swim. He gets a float, but the duckling meets
up with Tom, who plans to cook him. Jerry
intervenes and hits Tom full in the face with
a shovel. Tom is forced into the shape of a
buckled tube. Jerry gives him a swollen
head by blowing through the tube, and the
duckling bursts this giant cat head with the
prick of a safety pin. Tom locks Jerry up in a
can. He starts out after the duckling and falls
in the water. He begins to drown. The duckling rescues him, and Jerry warms up poor,
frozen Tom.

The duckling follows his siblings in an
athletic swimming style.

Note
• **Musical score: "Love That Pup" (Bradley).**

1953

Two Little Indians

Directors: William Hanna,
Joseph Barbera
Producer: Fred Quimby
(Metro-Goldwyn-Mayer)
Animation: Ray Patterson, Kenneth
Muse, Irven Spence, Ed Barge
Music: Scott Bradley
Set Design: Robert Gentle
Technicolor (6 min. 49 sec.)

Jerry, a scout chief, is asked to take charge of two little orphaned mice. But the two little mice, dressed up as Indians, have no sense of danger. One of them gets caught by Spike. Fortunately, Jerry snatches them away from the dog. The other mouse aims his bow and arrow at a bird. Jerry rushes in, scolds him, and gets an arrow in his rear. The two little mice attack Tom, but Spike captures Jerry, and the two mice set him free. Tom gets scalped, and is knocked out by Jerry and by a mailbox that falls on him. The three mice scamper away, and Tom tears himself apart going after them. Tom

Notes

- Musical score: "Love That Pup" (Bradley).
- When Tom's body comes apart chasing after the mice, his head, paws, and body go off in three different directions.

captures Jerry. The two little mice send up smoke signals from the toaster. One of them paints Indian heads on some badminton shuttlecocks. Tom, dressed as Davy Crockett, gets ready to raise a siege against these "assailants." The two little mice disguise Spike as an Indian chief. Tom is horrified at the sight of him. One of the little mice climbs into Tom's rifle and shoots an arrow at him. The other mouse sets fire to the gunpowder, and the house explodes. Tom gives up.

The three mice smoke a peace pipe. Tom smokes, too, but he swallows the smoke and chokes.

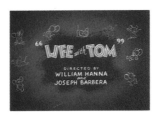

1953

LIFE WITH TOM

Directors: William Hanna,
Joseph Barbera
Producer: Fred Quimby
(Metro-Goldwyn-Mayer)
Animation: Kenneth Muse, Irven
Spence, Ed Barge
Music: Scott Bradley
Set Design: Robert Gentle
Technicolor (7 min. 49 sec.)

J erry receives a package. Tom grabs it and opens it. It's a book, *Life with Tom,* by Jerry Mouse. It's a bestseller written by Jerry. Tom starts to read it.

Chapter VII: Tom goes fishing and uses Jerry as bait. Jerry attaches the line to Spike's paw. Tom casts Spike out on his rod and Spike retaliates. (Excerpt from "Cat Fishin'," 1947.)

Tom discovers that the cats in the neighborhood are enjoying Jerry's book. He is furious, but he continues to read.

Chapter XI: Tom, disguised as an Indian, confronts Jerry and Nibbles. He's hit in the face with a champagne cork, then with a pie. His tail catches on fire from candle-arrows, and he's finally catapulted into the air by a champagne bottle. Exhausted and beaten, he surrenders. (Excerpt from "The Little Orphan," 1949.)

Tom passes by Spike and Tyke, laughing as they read. He continues his own reading.

Chapter XX: Tom ties Jerry to the tracks of a toy train and, perched on the motor carriage, drives the train toward him. But the canary appears and throws a bowling ball, which derails the train. Tom is buried with the train, in a hole. (From "Kitty Foiled," 1948.)

Tom is furious. He shows Jerry the book that has just come out and hits him. Jerry shows him the letter from the publisher and a check for $25,000, with 50 percent of the royalties meant for Tom. Tom is the first to laugh.

Notes

• **Musical score: "Love That Pup" (Bradley), "Here Comes the Sun" (Woods–Freed), "The Trolley Song" (Martin–Blane).**

• **This film is the only one of the series in which Spike, Tyke, and Nibbles all appear at the same time.**

1954

PUPPY TALE

Directors: William Hanna,
Joseph Barbera
Producer: Fred Quimby
(Metro-Goldwyn-Mayer)
Animation: Ed Barge, Irven Spence,
Kenneth Muse
Music: Scott Bradley
Set Design: John Didrik Johnsen
Technicolor (7 min. 3 sec.)

It's nighttime. A car pulls up on a bridge, and a sack is thrown into the river. Jerry takes it out of the water. Five dogs and a puppy escape. Jerry tries in vain to chase the puppy away, and then decides to take him home. The puppy drinks Tom's milk. Tom puts the puppy out of the house, but Jerry lets him in again. The puppy falls asleep in Tom's basket and gets thrown out again. The puppy gets into an empty milk bottle. Jerry lets him inside the house again. Tom swings into action, and the puppy soon finds himself outside, with Jerry. Tom begins to feel guilty when he sees the rainstorm outside, and he imagines Jerry and the puppy drowning. He decides to let them back in, but when he goes looking for them, he falls into a puddle. Jerry and the pup rescue him and warm him up. Finally, all three are snug and warm inside the house, when the five other dogs arrive, responding to the pup's bark. All the dogs descend on Tom's milk bowl.

Note
• Musical score: "Love That Pup" (Bradley), "Sleepy Head" (Donaldson–Kahn).

POSSE CAT

Directors: William Hanna,
Joseph Barbera
Producer: Fred Quimby
(Metro-Goldwyn-Mayer)
Animation: Irven Spence, Ed Barge,
Kenneth Muse, Ray Patterson
Music: Scott Bradley
Set Design: Robert Gentle
Technicolor (6 min. 28 sec.)

Jerry gets hold of a sausage. The ranch cook offers Tom a number of dishes, saying that he can't have them until he captures Jerry. Tom tries to catch him, but Jerry lassoes him. Tom throws his lasso, but instead of catching Jerry, he gets the turkey that the cook was putting in the oven. The cook gets angry and draws a gun on Tom.

Jerry prepares a sandwich with the cook's hand as the meat. Tom bites it and the cook immediately shoots him. The water Tom drinks starts coming out of the holes in his skin.

Jerry then makes a sandwich with a bull! Tom takes a bite and the bull, in a rage, sends him flying.

Jerry then offers to go fifty-fifty with Tom on all his future meals. Tom accepts. He pretends to be a fierce cowboy by twirling his revolvers, and as a reward gets a big meal, which he refuses to share with Jerry. So the mouse pitches the plate and its contents right in his face. Tom goes after him, with a red-hot brand, but gets the cook, not Jerry. Tom runs away, pursued by the cook, who is firing away at him. Meanwhile, Jerry eats in peace.

Notes

• **Musical score: "Love That Pup" (Bradley), "Making Love, Mountain Style" (School–Moulton).**

• **Tom, hit by the cook's gun, drinks some water, which streams out of the holes. The same device was used in "Hatch Up Your Troubles" (1949).**

HIC-CUP PUP

Directors: William Hanna,
Joseph Barbera
Producer: Fred Quimby
(Metro-Goldwyn-Mayer)
Animation: Ed Barge, Kenneth Muse,
Ray Patterson, Irven Spence
Music: Scott Bradley
Set Design: Robert Gentle
Technicolor (6 min. 17 sec.)

Spike is putting his son Tyke to sleep. He places him in his cradle and demands immediate silence from a chirping bird. Tom comes along, on his way after Jerry. Spike warns him: "If you wake up my son. . . ." Tyke has the hiccups. Spike sternly warns Tom: "Don't you wake him again!" But Jerry bites Tom, and Tom, now chasing after Jerry, hits Spike with a shovel. Tyke still has the hiccups. Tom gets his hand caught in a mousetrap. He whistles into a garden hose and makes a noise like a trumpet. Spike is getting angrier by the minute.

Tyke still has the hiccups; Tom now gets them, followed by Spike. Spike tries to get rid of Tyke's hiccups by frightening him. Tom falls off the roof while chasing Jerry. He buries himself underground, convinced of Spike's inevitable reaction. But Tyke and Spike no longer have the hiccups. Spike thanks Tom. They are now reconciled. Jerry, disgusted, leaves for the South.

Notes

• **Musical score: "Love That Pup" (Bradley).**

• **The film's original title was "Tyke Takes a Nap."**

LITTLE SCHOOL MOUSE

Directors: William Hanna,
Joseph Barbera
Producer: Fred Quimby
(Metro-Goldwyn-Mayer)
Animation: Irven Spence, Ed Barge
Music: Scott Bradley
Set Design: Robert Gentle
Technicolor (7 min. 50 sec.)

We are in mouse school. Tuffy is at his desk. It's ten after nine. Jerry, the teacher, arrives late, because Tom has been chasing him.

Jerry teaches Tuffy how to avoid a cat's paw. He uses a mechanical paw for the demonstration, but Jerry gets crushed by the paw he's supposed to be avoiding. The first test is to pull off a cat's whiskers without awakening him. Jerry does it successfully, but Tuffy pulls on Tom along with the whiskers. Tom strikes Jerry. The second test is grabbing a piece of cheese without awaken-

ing the cat. Jerry succeeds in stealing a small piece of cheese, but Tuffy asks Tom to give him the enormous piece that he's not able to reach. The third test consists of putting a bell on the cat. Jerry ties a little bell around Tom's neck, but Tom hits back. Tuffy presents Tom with a little bell, and Tom is only too happy to wear it around his neck. Jerry throws his teaching license away, and Tuffy begins teaching cats and mice to be good friends. Tom and Jerry listen.

1954

BABY BUTCH

Directors: William Hanna,
Joseph Barbera
Producer: Fred Quimby
(Metro-Goldwyn-Mayer)
Animation: Irven Spence, Kenneth
Muse, Ed Barge
Music: Scott Bradley
Set Design: Vera Ohman
Technicolor (7 min. 9 sec.)

Butch, a black street cat, is looking for food. He sees that the refrigerator in the house where Tom lives is full, and he makes believe he's a starving, abandoned baby. Tom takes him in. Butch tries to steal a ham, but Tom gives him a bottle instead. Butch knocks him out, but Tom recovers and helps the "baby" burp at the end of his meal. Jerry comes along and takes the ham. Butch strikes again. Tom gives Butch a bath. Butch shows him that Jerry has laid his paws on the ham. Tom takes the ham back and discovers the baby hidden in the refrigerator.

Jerry gets the ham back, but Butch completely empties the refrigerator. He hits Tom and grabs the ham. Thanks to Jerry, the food stays in the house and Butch finds himself back outside. Tom and Jerry share the ham. Butch reappears. He cuts himself a slice of ham and tries to devour the rest. Tom and Jerry jump on him.

Note
• Musical score: "Love That Pup" (Bradley), "I Got Out of Bed on the Right Side" (Schwartz–Mercer).

"Baby Butch"

MICE FOLLIES

Directors: William Hanna,
Joseph Barbera
Producer: Fred Quimby
(Metro-Goldwyn-Mayer)
Animation: Kenneth Muse, Ed Barge,
Irven Spence, Ray Patterson
Music: Scott Bradley
Technicolor (6 min. 49 sec.)

Jerry and Tuffy, who have turned on the water, cause the kitchen and bathroom sink to overflow, and then freeze the water with a refrigerator electrode. Jerry dances on the ice. He dances with Tuffy. Tom arrives, and Tuffy hooks on to his whiskers. Jerry cuts Tom's claws, and the cat is sent flying far out into the distance by the two mice.

But Tom finds a pair of ice skates. Now he's able to compete and toy with his two opponents on the ice. Tom chases Jerry, passes under a door, and comes out looking suddenly like a toboggan. Tuffy makes a springboard and Tom goes flying off into the air. He lands in the cellar. He reappears, armed with a syphon, tracking down Jerry. Tuffy melts the ice, then refreezes it at a single blow. Tom is frozen into the ice, and Jerry dances around the icy cat.

Note

• Musical score: "Love That Pup" (Bradley), "Sleeping Beauty Waltz" (Tchaikovsky).

NEAPOLITAN MOUSE

Directors: William Hanna,
Joseph Barbera
Producer: Fred Quimby
(Metro-Goldwyn-Mayer)
Animation: Ed Barge, Irven Spence,
Ray Patterson, Kenneth Muse
Music: Scott Bradley
Set Design: John Didrik Johnsen
Technicolor (7 min. 15 sec.)

Tom and Jerry arrive in Naples, Italy. Tom chases Jerry but is defeated, temporarily. The chase continues. Tom attacks Jerry with a frying pan. Topo, an Italian mouse, arrives on the scene. He knocks out Tom and helps Jerry. Tom is transformed into an accordion by a blue dog. Topo comes to his aid and ties up the dog. Topo recognizes his two new friends, Tom and Jerry, as the famous cartoon heroes. He takes them on a tour of Naples, showing them the San Carlo Opera House and Mount Vesuvius. But the blue dog reappears, accompanied by two other dogs. Tom, Jerry, and Topo send three big cheeses rolling after the dogs, and they land in the water. The ship's siren blows: It's time to go. Tom and Jerry leave. Topo and the three Neapolitan dogs say farewell.

Notes

• Musical score: "My Friend Dodo" (Bradley), "Oh Marie" (DiCapua).

• Given the original script and the music entitled "My Friend Dodo," it appears that the Neapolitan mouse was named Dodo, before becoming "Topo" (which means mouse in Italian).

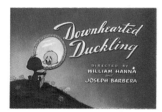

1954

DOWNHEARTED DUCKLING

Directors: William Hanna,
Joseph Barbera
Producer: Fred Quimby
(Metro-Goldwyn-Mayer)
Animation: Irven Spence, Ray
Patterson, Kenneth Muse, Ed Barge
Music: Scott Bradley
Set Design: Robert Gentle
Technicolor (6 min. 42 sec.)

A duckling is crying. Jerry arrives. The duckling shows him *The Ugly Duckling,* which he's been reading. He wants to kill himself with an ax. Jerry saves him. The duckling asks Tom to eat him. Tom, delighted by this request, obeys, but Jerry interferes and snatches the duckling away in the nick of time. The duckling then settles inside a sandwich meant for Tom. Jerry again snatches the duckling out of Tom's grasp. Jerry, thinking he has hold of the duckling, actually has a hen.

The duckling hides in a pie, hoping that Tom will eat it, but Jerry arrives and throws the pie in Tom's face. Jerry gives the duckling a beauty treatment, but Tom is horrified at the sight of him.

The duckling grows sadder by the minute and pulls a sack over his head. Along comes a female duckling, who talks to the duckling and finds him handsome. Jerry rejoices at this turn of events. The duckling and his new girlfriend leave together!

Note

• **Musical score: "Love That Pup" (Bradley), "It's a Most Unusual Day" (McHugh–Adamson).**

1954

PET PEEVE

Directors: William Hanna,
Joseph Barbera
Producer: Fred Quimby
(Metro-Goldwyn-Mayer)
Animation: Ed Barge, Irven Spence,
Kenneth Muse
Music: Scott Bradley
Set Design: Robert Gentle
Technicolor (6 mins. 35 sec.)

Spike is preparing a huge sandwich for himself. So is Tom. Together, they eat up their masters' food. Their masters realize they have too many expenses, and that the animals' food is costing too much. They decide to get rid of one of them. Tom immediately snuggles up to his mistress, slyly—and cynically—playing with a ball of wool. Spike, begins licking his master effusively. Tom does housework, vacuuming and dusting the furniture, while Spike does the ironing. The mistress of the house tells her husband that a cat can do something that's

Notes

- Musical score: "Love That Pup" (Bradley).
- The influence of the UPA style is especially clear in the line drawing, which characterizes the representation of Tom and Spike. We've come a long way from "Mammy Two Shoes."

impossible for a dog: catch a mouse. The husband accepts the challenge: The animal that will catch Jerry can remain.

Tom and Spike break into a mad chase after the mouse, and each one grabs Jerry from the other as he catches him. Tom pretends to be beaten and to leave, but puts Spike out the door. Spike sees he's been fooled and returns. Tom and Spike chase each other and fight a duel, destroying the house in the process.

The masters decide to keep only Jerry. Tom and Spike take to their heels, and carry off the refrigerator!

Touché, Pussy Cat!

Directors: William Hanna,
Joseph Barbera
Producer: Fred Quimby
(Metro-Goldwyn-Mayer)
Animation: Kenneth Muse, Ed Barge,
Irven Spence
Music: Scott Bradley
Set Design: Robert Gentle
Technicolor (6 min. 45 sec.)

Tuffy arrives in Paris and goes to the mouseketeers' headquarters. Captain Jerry reads the letter of recommendation from his friend François Mouse, about his young son Tuffy. Jerry supervises Tuffy's training, but the impetuous Tuffy breaks everything he touches and sticks Jerry with his sword. Tuffy pays court to a young lady mouse who steps over Jerry in order to avoid dirtying herself in a mud puddle. Tuffy provokes Tom, and Jerry cuts the cat's tail into circles. Jerry writes to François Mouse that his son will never make a real mouseketeer. Tuffy leaves, dejected.

Tom and Jerry fight a duel. Tuffy flies to the aid of Captain Jerry. He cuts Tom's tail, then draws a cat on the wall, singing "Frère Jacques" as he works. Tom appears and Tuffy draws a pair of glasses on Tom's face. Tuffy fires at Tom with a cork from a champagne bottle and opens a barrel that washes Tom away into the nearest sewer. "Poor, poor pussy cat," says Tuffy ironically. Jerry makes Tuffy a mousketeer but the little mouse again sticks him with his sword and gets a spanking from Jerry. "C'est la guerre!" Tuffy admits in French.

Notes

- Musical score: "We're on Our Way" (Brown–Brent).

- The film was nominated for an Academy Award. This was the last nomination that the series received.

1955

SOUTHBOUND DUCKLING

Directors: William Hanna,
Joseph Barbera
Producer: Fred Quimby
(Metro-Goldwyn-Mayer)
Animation: Kenneth Muse, Ed Barge,
Irven Spence
Music: Scott Bradley
Set Design: Vera Ohman
Tracing: Dick Bickenbach
Technicolor (6 min. 15 sec.)

The duckling is getting ready to go south. He packs his valise and says goodbye to Jerry, who tries in vain to make him understand that he's a domestic duck, not a migratory bird. The duckling tries, with no success, to catch up with other migratory ducks. He can't even get off the ground.

The duckling uses a sling to launch his flight, but he ends up in Tom's mouth. Tom opens a cookbook, *How to Cook a Duck*. The duckling uses a board to propel himself into the air. A weight falls on the board, and the duckling flies up but soon falls down again into Tom's frying pan. Jerry rescues him. The duckling sits himself on a rocket. The rocket goes off. Tom swallows the rocket, but not the duck. The duckling finally uses a balloon to get into the air. Tom aims a gun at it, but Jerry rescues the duckling again. Jerry and the duckling leave together for the south—by plane. But Tom

goes along, crouching against the landing gear. Jerry and the duckling relax on the beach, but suddenly Tom appears and catches them, imprisoning them beneath a bucket.

Note
- Musical score: "Love That Pup" (Bradley).

1 9 5 5

PUP ON A PICNIC

Directors: William Hanna,
Joseph Barbera
Producer: Fred Quimby
(Metro-Goldwyn-Mayer)
Animation: Ray Patterson, Kenneth
Muse, Ed Barge, Irven Spence
Music: Scott Bradley
Set Design: Robert Gentle
Technicolor (7 min. 4 sec.)

Spike and his son Tyke are preparing a picnic basket. But Tom is in pursuit of Jerry and, in the heat of the chase, upsets the basket's contents. The two dogs set off for the forest with their basket, with Jerry perched on top. Tom grabs a string of sausages, thinking the two dogs are chasing Jerry. Spike catches up with him, but Tom throws out a sausage, and the dog runs after it. He then sees that he's been tricked. Tom goes after Jerry, who is hidden in a sandwich. Jerry makes Spike believe that Tom has thrown a tomato at him. Spike chases after Tom but Tom manages to lose the dog, who has been biting his leg. Tom soon finds himself stuck in a tree. He takes this opportunity to fish out the food from the basket with a fishing rod. But a column of ants arrives and sees the food. They climb the tree

while Tom is fishing out Jerry. The ants reach him, causing the apple tree to drop all its fruit to the ground, burying the two dogs and Tom. The ants leave again with the food and with Jerry, still hiding inside a sandwich.

Note
• **Musical score: "Love That Pup" (Bradley), "I'll Make a Happy Landing" (McHugh–Fields).**

MOUSE FOR SALE

Directors: William Hanna,
Joseph Barbera
Producer: Fred Quimby
(Metro-Goldwyn-Mayer)
Animation: Kenneth Muse, Ed Barge,
Irven Spence, Ray Patterson
Music: Scott Bradley
Set Design: Robert Gentle
Technicolor (6 min. 48 sec.)

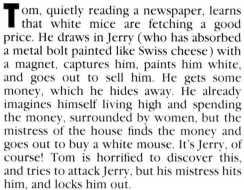

Tom, quietly reading a newspaper, learns that white mice are fetching a good price. He draws in Jerry (who has absorbed a metal bolt painted like Swiss cheese) with a magnet, captures him, paints him white, and goes out to sell him. He gets some money, which he hides away. He already imagines himself living high and spending the money, surrounded by women, but the mistress of the house finds the money and goes out to buy a white mouse. It's Jerry, of course! Tom is horrified to discover this, and tries to attack Jerry, but his mistress hits him, and locks him out.

Jerry puts on his act as "Jerry, the Dancing Mouse." Tom turns a garden hose on him, and Jerry soon becomes brown again. He runs off, through the teapot handle, plunges into the flour and becomes white again. Tom uses a bellows; Jerry is now half white and half brown. He behaves like a dancing girl, hiding his "nudity." Tom sets to work again, and Jerry is completely brown this time. He uses some white shoe polish, and reappears in white.

Tom gets disgusted and leaves. He covers himself with white paint and returns. He has become "Tom, the Dancing Cat." His mistress now allows him to reenter the house. Tom begins to dance, stepping regularly on Jerry.

Note

• Musical score: "Love That Pup" (Bradley), "Here's to the Girls" (Edens–Freed).

1955

DESIGNS ON JERRY

Directors: William Hanna,
Joseph Barbera
Producer: Fred Quimby
(Metro-Goldwyn-Mayer)
Animation: Irven Spence, Kenneth
Muse, Ed Barge
Music: Scott Bradley
Set Design: John Didrik Johnsen
Technicolor (6 min. 39 sec.)

Tom designs a sophisticated trap for Jerry. Exhausted by his work, he falls asleep and dreams that he's a rich industrialist, the head of Tom's Mouse Trap Factory.

The mouse in the design comes to life and wakes Jerry up. He erases the ferocious teeth of the cat in the design; and the cat comes to life. Jerry shortens the cat's paws, and quickly sketches a bow with which he can shoot arrows into the cat. The two mice flee, pursued by the cat, who's transformed into a cat on springs. The two mice change the number 10, which was one of the dimensions of the drawing, into 12. This simple change, unknown to Tom, will have amazing consequences. Tom builds the trap according to the measurements indicated. Jerry, in a very cocky frame of mind, grabs a piece of cheese, and the trap is set into motion.

Taking the piece of cheese triggers an alarm, which sets off a saw, which cuts a huge log. The cut part of the log then falls on a pair of scissors, which cuts a string, releasing a hammer. The hammer falls, and its weight sets a banana flying into a windshield. The windshield wiper is set into motion, and raises a mechanical hand, which pours a pail of water whose contents are deposited on a pair of scales. One of the scales sets off a ventilator, which pushes a vessel on which a billiard cue has been placed. The cue launches a ball, which hits a button and activates a washing machine, whose mechanism stretches a thread and sets off a gun, whose bullet divides the balance wheels of a clock, which reveals a cuckoo mounted on a knife. The knife cuts the cord from which hangs a safe. Tom, confident in his trap's success, calmly waits for the safe to fall, while Jerry, with his eyes blindfolded, smokes a last cigarette. But the safe falls on Tom and transforms him into a cube!

Notes

• Musical score: "Love That Pup" (Bradley).

• Certain shots from this film are reused in "Shutter Bugged Cat" (1967).

1955

TOM AND CHERIE

Directors: William Hanna,
Joseph Barbera
Producer: Fred Quimby
(Metro-Goldwyn-Mayer)
Animation: Irvin Spence, Kenneth
Muse, Lewis Marshall, Ed Barge
Music: Scott Bradley
Set Design: Robert Gentle
Tracing: Dick Bickenbach
Technicolor (6 min. 46 sec.)

Jerry, mouseketeer captain, is madly in love with lovely Lilli. He writes her a passionate letter, which the faithful Tuffy, a mouseketeer, is ordered to bring her. Tuffy blushes as he reads the letter, but on his way he meets Tom, one of the cardinal's guards, who challenges him with his sword. Tuffy returns and explains to Jerry that there's no way for him to pass. But a mouseketeer is always courageous, and Tuffy starts out again. He quickly returns, since Tom is still there. Tuffy leaves, sheltered under a helmet. When he discovers Tom there, he calls on Jerry for help. But Tom is knocked out by the helmet, and Jerry, on arriving, finds no one.

Tuffy is sentenced to writing "A mouseketeer is brave!" one hundred times on the blackboard. Tuffy finally manages to get the letter to Lilli, who sends another back with him. Tom appears and fights a duel with Tuffy, who manages to get back to Jerry and give him the letter. Jerry reads it and writes another, which Tuffy is supposed to deliver. Noise is heard. Tuffy returns in a sorry state. Jerry writes another letter. Tuffy leaves to deliver it. More noise. Tuffy returns again, completely done in. Lilli's last letter, delivered by Tuffy, says: "Our love is finished." Tuffy, however, is no better off, for Jerry has replaced Lilli's portrait by one of Marie, his new ladylove.

Tuffy leaves with a new letter. Tom challenges him, "En garde, en garde." But Tuffy, resigned, goes off into the distance.

Notes

• **Musical score: "Love That Pup" (Bradley).**

• **This is the third time Tom acts as a cardinal's guard, while Jerry and Tuffy are King's mouseketeers.**

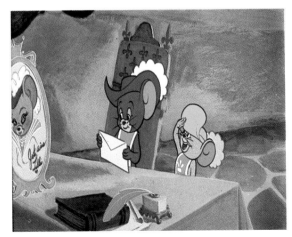

1955

SMARTY CAT

Directors: William Hanna,
Joseph Barbera
Producer: Fred Quimby
(Metro-Goldwyn-Mayer)
Animation: Irven Spence, Kenneth
Muse, Ed Barge, Michael Lah
Music: Scott Bradley
Set Design: Vera Ohman
Tracing: Dick Bickenbach
Technicolor (6 min. 50 sec.)

Tom invites his three cat friends to the
house. The three cats (which include
Butch) arrive, and the four of them organize
a film showing. Tom chases after Jerry, who
is also there. The film, shot by Butch, is entitled "Tom the Terrific Cat."

Part One: "Lover Boy." Tom sees the
white kitten and whistles in admiration. He
hits Spike with a brick and kisses the kitten's
paw, then Spike's paw, who has taken her
place. All this time, he's been talking in his
Charles Boyer voice. Tom, who suddenly
discovers the truth, knocks Spike to the
ground (excerpt from "Solid Serenade,"
1946).

Jerry has returned to the house. Tom
starts chasing him again.

Part Two: "The Dumb Dog." Tom wants
to go fishing, but Spike is on guard. He enters the private estate. Spike mistakes Tom
for a bone (excerpt from "Cat Fishin',"
1947).

Jerry, who has returned, is chased by
Tom's friend, the black cat. Jerry invites
Spike to look at the next episode.

Part Three: "New Leash on Life." Tom
reads in the newspaper that from now on all
dogs will have to be tied up. He plays
around with Spike, who is attached, but who
still manages to hit him with a baseball bat
(excerpt from "Fit to Be Tied," 1952).

Suddenly, Spike appears and chases all
four cats out of the house. Jerry films the
scene.

Note

• **Musical score: "Love That Pup" (Bradley), "You Were
Meant for Me" (Brown—Freed), "Milkman, Keep These
Bottles Quiet" (Raye—DePaul), "That Old Feeling"
(Brown—Fain).**

SMARTY CAT

137

PECOS PEST

Directors: William Hanna,
Joseph Barbera
Producer: Fred Quimby
(Metro-Goldwyn-Mayer)
Animation: Ed Barge, Irven Spence,
Ray Patterson, Kenneth Muse
Music: Scott Bradley
Set Design: Robert Gentle
Technicolor (6 min. 35 sec.)

Uncle Pecos, Jerry's uncle from Texas, arrives at his nephew's house with his guitar. He is soon scheduled to make his debut on television, so he rehearses before his show. He sings "Froggie Went A-Courtin'." When one of his guitar strings breaks, he pulls out one of Tom's whiskers, and then a second one. Tom is furious and Jerry and his uncle take to their heels. But nothing stops his uncle, who pulls out still another whisker. Tom dons the helmet of a suit of armor, but Uncle Pecos manages to tear out another whisker. Tom, who is attacked with an ax by the uncle, resolves to give him one of his whiskers.

Tom and Jerry watch the rebroadcast of Uncle Pecos's number. He breaks one of his guitar strings as he plays. Tom begins laughing, but Uncle Pecos stretches his paw out of the television set and yanks another whisker out of the hypnotized Tom.

Notes

• Musical score: "Love That Pup" (Bradley), "Froggie Went A-Courtin'" (arr. George "Shug" Fisher; guitar improvisation: Fisher).

• Fred Quimby's name appears on the series' credits for the last time. From now on William Hanna and Joseph Barbera produce their own films.

• "Shug" Fisher belonged to the group known as "Sons of the Pioneers." He had been seen in John Ford's "Rio Grande" (1950)

THAT'S MY MOMMY

Directors: William Hanna,
Joseph Barbera
Producers: William Hanna, Joseph
Barbera (Metro-Goldwyn-Mayer)
Animation: Kenneth Muse, Ed Barge,
Irvin Spence, Lewis Marshall
Music: Scott Bradley
Set Design: Robert Gentle
Tracing: Dick Bickenbach
Technicolor (6 min. 3 sec.)

An egg from a duck's brood rolls over to Tom's paws. The duckling hatches out of the egg and mistakes Tom for his mommy. "My Mommy, my dear sweet Mommy," he says. Tom, delighted by his luck, ties the duckling up, intending to roast him over the fire. Jerry steps in, rescues the duckling, and places Tom's tail over the fire instead. But the duckling comes back to Tom. The cat prepares a pastry crust, wraps it around the duckling, and puts him in the oven. Jerry steps in again and hits Tom on the head with a broom. The duckling revives Tom and gives him a kiss. Tom spreads fat over the duckling and puts some potatoes and carrots with him into the oven. Jerry opens the oven with a can opener and saves the duckling, who begins hitting him.

Jerry shows the duckling a book in which there's a picture of a duck and a cat. The duckling closes the book on Jerry, flattening him. Tom catches Jerry, imprisons him in a series of boxes, and throws him down a well. But the duckling finally begins to understand—Tom wants to cook him.

He is prepared to throw himself into the boiling water of his own free will. Tom,

deeply moved, rescues him, and his tears turn into a torrent. Jerry comes out of the well and sees the duckling swimming about after Tom, who is behaving like a mother duck.

Notes

• Musical score: "Love That Pup" (Bradley).

• William Hanna and Joseph Barbera are now, for the first time, their own producers.

THE FLYING SORCERESS

Directors: William Hanna,
Joseph Barbera
Producers: William Hanna, Joseph
Barbera (Metro-Goldwyn-Mayer)
Animation: Ed Barge, Irvin Spence,
Lewis Marshall, Kenneth Muse
Music: Scott Bradley
Set Design: Robert Gentle
Tracing: Dick Bickenbach
Technicolor (6 min. 40 sec.)

Tom and Jerry are at it again. The mistress of the house, a young brunette, scolds Tom and makes him clean up the house with a broom. Dejected, Tom reads a want ad placed by an old lady who is looking for a traveling companion. He goes to the address given—13 Sunnydale Road—and discovers a big, grim house, beset by thunder and lightning.

He enters and finds a witch perched on a broom. She makes him take a ride through the air on her broom, cackling as she goes. Tom jumps off the broom. The witch catches him and hires him as her companion.

Left alone, Tom mounts the broom, but is soon stopped by a tree branch. Jerry sees it passing across the sky and is amazed. But the witch steps in and makes Tom take a "trip," during which he's put through the mill. Tom wakes up and finds he's being shaken by the young mistress of the house. He was having a dream, with his head leaning against the broom. Tom sits astride the broom, which takes off into the air. The mistress of the house and Jerry watch him depart up into the sky!

Notes

• Musical score: "Love That Pup" (Bradley).

• Some shots from this film were reused in "Matinee Mouse" (1966).

• Contrary to custom, the face of Tom's owner is in full view.

THE EGG AND JERRY

Directors: William Hanna,
Joseph Barbera
Producers: William Hanna, Joseph
Barbera (Metro-Goldwyn-Mayer)
Animation: Ed Barge, Ray Patterson,
Irven Spence, Kenneth Muse
Music: Scott Bradley
Set Design: Don Driscoll
Tracing: Dick Bickenbach
Technicolor. CinemaScope (7 min.
50 sec.)

This is a CinemaScope remake of "Hatch Up Your Troubles" (1949).

"Hatch Up Your Troubles"

"The Egg and Jerry"

Notes

• This is the first of three CinemaScope versions. The only changes from the original are the settings, which are simpler and more schematic, and the colors, which are harsher.

• The name of Fred Quimby has disappeared, and those of Don Driscoll and Dick Bickenbach have been added.

1 9 5 6

BUSY BUDDIES

Directors: William Hanna,
Joseph Barbera
Producers: William Hanna, Joseph
Barbera (Metro-Goldwyn-Mayer)
Animation: Irvin Spence, Lewis
Marshall, Kenneth Muse, Ed Barge
Music: Scott Bradley
Set Design: Robert Gentle
Tracing: Dick Bickenbach
Technicolor. CinemaScope (6 min.
15 sec.)

A couple go out for the evening and leave their baby with a young babysitter, Jeannie. As soon as the parents have left, Jeannie gets on the telephone. Jerry, meanwhile, eats some cake, and Tom finishes off a watermelon. Tom and Jerry suddenly see the baby, who crawls across the sink and falls in. Tom catches him in the nick of time and puts him back in his bed. Jeannie continues her telephone conversation. The baby sets out again. He falls down into the cellar and starts crawling about amidst the pipes. He emerges completely black. Tom cleans him up, but Jeannie scolds Tom and throws a book at him, thinking that he's annoying the baby.

The baby gets out of bed, climbs the staircase, goes prowling about on the curtain rod, and slides off. Jerry catches him.

The baby gets out through the mail drop, into the big postbox in the street. Tom and Jerry open it with a can opener and retrieve the baby. They put him back in bed.

The couple return. Jeannie declares that there's been no problem with the baby. Her only complaint is about Tom!

Notes

- Musical score: "Love That Pup" (Bradley).

- The characters of Jeannie, the negligent babysitter, and the roving baby appear for the first time in this film; they will be seen again in "Tot Watchers" (1958).

- The master and mistress of the house are completely visible; their faces are not hidden, as they had formerly been.

MUSCLE BEACH TOM

Directors: William Hanna,
Joseph Barbera
Producers: William Hanna, Joseph
Barbera (Metro-Goldwyn-Mayer)
Animation: Lewis Marshall, Kenneth
Muse, Ed Barge, Irvin Spence
Music: Scott Bradley
Set Design: Robert Gentle
Tracing: Dick Bickenbach
Technicolor. CinemaScope (6 min.
45 sec.)

The scene is a beach, where several cats are exercising. Tom arrives with his kitten girlfriend. Tom puts his things down on top of Jerry, who arrived earlier. Jerry is annoyed. He's covered with trash. He's fed up and strikes Tom with a banana. Tom, enraged, first blows him up into a balloon, then throws him way out to sea.

Tom is fascinated by Butch, an athletic black cat. Butch chases Tom away. Tom, hit by a mast, winds up looking like a crab. He decides to show his rival how strong he is. He gets caught between two metal disks.

The kitten dances with Butch and Jerry. Jerry is dressed in a banana skin. Tom digs a hole and punches Butch into it. He then dances with the kitten, but Butch reappears. Butch sends Tom flying into a trash can. Tom uses some balloons in order to pass himself off as a strong, tough guy. He attacks Butch with an anchor, which prevents Tom from flying off. He strikes Jerry, too, but the mouse unties the anchor, and Tom ascends into the air. Jerry shows off like a tough mouse in front of the white kitten, but gets crushed between two tomatoes.

Note
 Musical score: "Love That Pup" (Bradley).

DOWNBEAT BEAR

Directors: William Hanna,
Joseph Barbera
Producers: William Hanna, Joseph
Barbera (Metro-Goldwyn-Mayer)
Animation: Kenneth Muse, Ed Barge,
Irvin Spence, Lewis Marshall
Music: Scott Bradley
Set Design: Robert Gentle
Tracing: Dick Bickenbach
Technicolor. CinemaScope (6 min.
22 sec.)

Jerry comes home and turns on the radio. The music disturbs Tom. The radio announces that a dancing bear has escaped from a circus. His capture will be amply rewarded.

The bear arrives and does some dance steps. He steals some fruit and eats it. Tom, seeing this, tries to telephone the authorities, but Jerry turns on the music-playing radio again. The bear rushes over to Tom and leads him into a mad dance. Tom turns off the radio, but Jerry switches it on. The bear still wants to go on dancing with Tom. Tom cuts the radio wire with a pair of scissors. Jerry puts on a record player and the bear dances a passionate tango with Tom. Tom breaks the record over Jerry's head.

The mouse dances on the piano and begins playing the guitar. The bear falls into the cellar. The radio announces that the reward has been doubled. The bear reappears and wants to dance with Tom, but gets cornered by the daybed. Tom, now outdoors, turns off the transistor radio and throws it away. The radio catches on a tree branch and begins to play six hours of uninterrupted music. The bear invites Tom to dance, and the cat agrees.

Note
• Musical score: "Love That Pup" (Bradley), "La Cumparsita" (Rodriguez).

BLUE CAT BLUES

Directors: William Hanna,
Joseph Barbera
Producers: William Hanna, Joseph
Barbera (Metro-Goldwyn-Mayer)
Animation: Ed Barge, Irvin Spence,
Lewis Marshall, Kenneth Muse
Music: Scott Bradley
Set Design: Robert Gentle
Tracing: Dick Bickenbach
Technicolor. CinemaScope (6 min.
48 sec.)

Tom is down at the railroad tracks, bent on committing suicide. Jerry, who's there, too, tells us why.

Tom and Jerry were inseparable friends until the arrival of a voluptuous white kitten. Jerry tried to restrain Tom, who became the kitten's plaything, but it was no use. The kitten had Tom push her to and fro on a swing. Then Tom acquired a rival: Butch, the black cat. Butch had also noticed the kitten. He kissed her and got rid of Tom. Tom's gifts seemed poor compared to those of Butch. Tom had spent every penny he owned for a car; he'd agreed to pay for it in 312 monthly installments, with interest at 112 percent a year; he'd pledged an arm and a leg, and twenty years of his own life. But all that meant nothing compared to Butch's luxurious car. Tom started to drink. Jerry had, nevertheless, managed to pull him out of the gutter. Then Butch and the white kitten got married. Such was Tom's sad story. Jerry observes, with satisfaction, that he'd never had this problem, but suddenly he sees the mouse he loves passing by, with her fiancé. Jerry is desperate, as desperate as Tom. We hear the sound of an approaching train.

Note
• Musical score: "Love That Pup" (Bradley), "I've Got a Feelin' You're Foolin' " (Brown–Freed).

1 9 5 6

BARBECUE BRAWL

Directors: William Hanna,
Joseph Barbera
Producers: William Hanna, Joseph
Barbera (Metro-Goldwyn-Mayer)
Animation: Ed Barge, Irvin Spence,
Lewis Marshall, Kenneth Muse
Music: Scott Bradley
Set Design: Robert Gentle
Tracing: Dick Bickenbach
Technicolor. CinemaScope (6 min.
34 sec.)

Spike and his son Tyke are preparing a delicious barbecue. Spike grills an enormous steak, which shrinks to almost nothing after cooking. Jerry, chased by Tom, hides amidst the coals. Tom searches for him and breaks everything as he does so. Spike chases him away.

Tom pursues Jerry and falls into the pool. He hits Spike while looking for Jerry. Spike, furious, hits Tom with a shovel. From the shock of it, Tom seems completely confused. Jerry hides in the salad. Tom grabs him and falls into the salad bowl. Spike chases him away. Jerry hides in the pepper shaker and sneezes. He then hides in the bread, and Spike sees the bread moving, like a snake. Tom grabs the bread and hits Spike. He falls into the pool and comes out dripping.

Spike and Tyke prepare to eat, but an army of ants comes along. The two dogs fall into the water, while the ants carry all the food away, including the big steak that Spike unsuccessfully tried to save.

Note

- Musical score: "Love That Pup" (Bradley).

1 9 5 7

TOPS WITH POPS

Directors: William Hanna,
Joseph Barbera
Producers: William Hanna, Joseph
Barbera (Metro-Goldwyn-Mayer)
Animation: Ed Barge, Ray Patterson,
Irvin Spence, Kenneth Muse
Music: Scott Bradley
Set Design: Don Driscoll
Tracing: Dick Bickenbach
Technicolor. CinemaScope (7 min.
55 sec.)

This film is a CinemaScope remake of
"Love That Pup" (1949).

"Love That Pup"

"Tops with Pops"

Notes

• The name of Fred Quimby, who produced the first version, is no longer listed in the credits. The names of Don Driscoll and of Dick Bickenbach have been added. The animators, whose original work is used again, are the same. Once again, the settings of the first version, rendered with great care, differ considerably from the more schematic ones of this version.

• We note also that the two dogs, named Butch and Pup in "Love That Pup," have now become Spike and Tyke.

1957

TIMID TABBY

Directors: William Hanna,
Joseph Barbera
Producers: William Hanna, Joseph
Barbera (Metro-Goldwyn-Mayer)
Animation: Lewis Marshall, Kenneth
Muse, Irvin Spence, Ken Southworth,
Bill Schipek
Music: Scott Bradley
Set Design: Roberta Greutert
Tracing: Dick Bickenbach
Technicolor. CinemaScope (6 min.
49 sec.)

Tom receives a letter from his cousin
George, announcing his arrival and re-
minding him of his fear of mice. George arrives and is really frightened. Tom winds up
a mechanical mouse. George is terrified, and
Tom makes fun of him. Jerry comes out of
his mouse hole. George sees him and immediately hits the ceiling. He turns to water
and slithers down the drain. Jerry eats some
candy. Tom hits him. George reappears and
sees Jerry inside the television set, which
has been set down right in front of his hole.
Jerry makes horrible faces, and George gets
terribly upset. Each time Jerry frightens
George, he gets a blow from Tom. He no
longer understands what is happening and
soon sees himself chased by a double cat.
Exhausted, Jerry leaves for a rest home for
mice with nervous breakdowns.

Note

- Musical score: "Love That Pup" (Bradley).

1957

FEEDIN' THE KIDDIE

Directors: William Hanna,
Joseph Barbera
Producers: William Hanna, Joseph
Barbera (Metro-Goldwyn-Mayer)
Animation: Irvin Spence, Kenneth
Muse, Ed Barge, Ray Patterson
Music: Scott Bradley
Set Design: Don Driscoll
Tracing: Dick Bickenbach
Technicolor. CinemaScope (7 min.
40 sec.)

This film is a CinemaScope version of "The
Little Orphan" (1949).

Notes

- This is the last of three CinemaScope remakes.

- Quimby's name is no longer listed in the credits. The
names of Don Driscoll and Dick Bickenbach appear, and
the four animators remain the same.

- The little mouse, who was called Nibbles in "The Little Orphan," is now named Tuffy.

- Mammy Two Shoes, who put in a very brief appearance in the first version, has now disappeared.

- The sets are more stylized, and the colors are
harsher than those of "The Little Orphan."

1957

MUCHO MOUSE

Directors: William Hanna,
Joseph Barbera
Producers: William Hanna, Joseph
Barbera (Metro-Goldwyn-Mayer)
Animation: Lewis Marshall, Kenneth
Muse, Bill Schipek, Jack Carr, Ken
Southworth, Herman Cohen
Music: Scott Bradley
Set Design: Robert Gentle
Tracing: Ed Benedict, Dick
Bickenbach
Technicolor. CinemaScope (7 min. 4
sec.)

The setting is a Spanish town. Butch, a ginger cat, is playing the guitar while El
Magnífico, a mouse (Jerry), dances and
grabs a piece of cheese. The mistress of the
house is upset about this. Butch has shown
himself to be incapable of catching El Magnífico, who escapes him each time. Butch
ends up falling into his guitar. He tells his
mistress, "Nobody can catch him."

The señorita shows him a telegram from
Tom, "Olympic, U.S. and World Champion
Mouse Catcher," announcing his arrival.
Tom arrives, covered with medals and tro-
phies. He politely tries out a few words in
Spanish, and the señorita leaves the house.
Tom sees El Magnífico. He catches the
mouse and throws him out, but the mouse
returns. While looking for him, Tom is shut
out of the house. Tom changes into a bull,
and El Magnífico becomes a bullfighter. Tom
knocks him out. The mouse challenges him
and makes him disappear inside his *muleta*.
Tom gets tangled up and ends up tied in
knots. Butch hails El Magnífico as the winner.

The señorita returns. She discovers the
two cats playing the guitar. Butch says,
"What did I tell you? No one can capture El
Magnífico." And meanwhile, El Magnífico
steals some food.

Notes

- Musical score: "España Cani" (Marquina; arr: Scott
Bradley).

- In this film we see the face of the dark-haired mistress of the house.

TOM'S PHOTO FINISH

Directors: William Hanna,
Joseph Barbera
Producers: William Hanna, Joseph
Barbera (Metro-Goldwyn-Mayer)
Animation: Kenneth Muse, Bill
Schipek, Lewis Marshall, Jack Carr,
Herman Cohen, Ken Southworth
Music: Scott Bradley
Set Design: Robert Gentle
Tracing: Dick Bickenbach
Technicolor. CinemaScope (6 min.
19 sec.)

Tom escapes the vigilance of the couple who are his masters and goes off to devour the chicken in the refrigerator. The man discovers the partly eaten chicken and is furious. He insists on knowing who is responsible: Tom, or Spike the dog. Tom, sensing danger, traces dog paws leading to the sleeping Spike, and puts the chicken next to the dog. Jerry takes a picture of Tom as he's committing this heinous deed. The immediate result is that Spike is thrown out and Tom receives the chicken as a reward for good conduct. But Jerry shows Tom one of the photograph's many copies, and Tom now has to tear them all up. He tears up his master's paper, in which one of the pictures had been placed. He throws away other copies, and the master, now completely exasperated, wants to throw him out. His wife intervenes, but Tom has to swallow the cake she's been making, since one of the famous pictures was baked inside it. Tom makes fun of the unhappy Spike, who is still outside. While trying to destroy one of the photographs, which Jerry has launched like a little paper plane, Tom almost cuts his master's throat. The master finally sees one of the pictures and discovers the truth. Tom is thrown out of the house, and Spike is allowed back in. Spike has the last laugh, as he sees Jerry's last photograph of Tom being thrown out of the house.

Notes

- Musical score: "Love That Pup" (Bradley).
- We see all of both master and mistress, including their faces.

HAPPY GO DUCKY

Directors: William Hanna,
Joseph Barbera
Producers: William Hanna, Joseph
Barbera (Metro-Goldwyn-Mayer)
Animation: Kenneth Muse, Bill
Schipek, Ken Southworth, Herman
Cohen, Lewis Marshall, James
Escalante
Music: Scott Bradley
Set Design: Roberta Greutert
Tracing: Dick Bickenbach
Technicolor. CinemaScope (6 min.
24 sec.)

It's Easter morning, and Tom and Jerry are fighting over an Easter egg, a present from the Easter Bunny. A duckling hatches out of the egg. He begins swimming in Tom's milk, then mounts the seahorse from the fish bowl, and takes a swim in the drinking water. Tom and Jerry find him a trifle too aggressive and shut him up in his box, but the duckling gets out. He takes a swim in the bathtub, then in the sink, shouting "Happy Easter." He sticks Tom in the behind with a knife and shouts "Touché, Pussy Cat!" Tom and Jerry, exasperated, put him back in his egg and send it to the Easter Bunny.

But the duckling returns. He takes a shower and floods the house. Tom and Jerry put him in the garden pool. He meets some other ducklings, with whom he immediately strikes up a friendship. Tom and Jerry soon find themselves in a completely flooded house, thanks to the duckling, who opened the garden hose directly into the house.

The house is invaded by the other ducklings and soon there are five: the gift duckling and his four friends—who all sing "Happy Easter" to Tom and Jerry, while enjoying a swim in the living room.

Notes

- Musical score: "Love That Pup" (Bradley).
- The original title of the film was "One Quack Mind."

1958

ROYAL CAT NAP

Directors: William Hanna,
Joseph Barbera
Producers: William Hanna, Joseph
Barbera (Metro-Goldwyn-Mayer)
Animation: Carlo Vinci, Lewis
Marshall, Kenneth Muse
Music: Scott Bradley
Set Design: Robert Gentle
Tracing: Dick Bickenbach
Technicolor. CinemaScope (6 min.
45 sec.)

The king is quietly asleep in his bed. Two mouseketeers, Jerry and Tuffy, arrive and fall upon the food set out on the table. Tuffy breaks a cup, and the noise awakens the king, who calls for the cat. Tom arrives. The king warns Tom: "One more sound, and off with his head!"

Tom is on his guard. Tuffy throws a vase. Tom catches it. He also catches the dishes. Jerry spreads some nails around. Tom gets stuck and runs screaming out of the castle. Jerry dances with a suit of armor. The king looks as though he may wake up. Tom puts corks in the king's ears, and when he awakens, puts him to sleep again by playing the violin.

Tom gets hit by an arrow shot by Tuffy. He screams out in pain. The king wakes up and condemns him to death, but Tuffy intervenes and sings "Frère Jacques" into the monarch's ear. The king falls asleep. Tom, Jerry, and Tuffy duel with swords. "C'est la guerre," says Tuffy, in French.

Notes
• Musical score: "Love That Pup" (Bradley), "Frère Jacques" (traditional).
• This is the last time that Tom plays a cardinal's guard and that Jerry and Tuffy play king's mouseketeers.

1958

THE VANISHING DUCK

Directors: William Hanna,
Joseph Barbera
Producers: William Hanna, Joseph
Barbera (Metro-Goldwyn-Mayer)
Animation: Lewis Marshall, Kenneth
Muse, Carlo Vinci, James Escalante
Music: Scott Bradley
Set Design: Robert Gentle
Tracing: Dick Bickenbach
Technicolor. CinemaScope (7 min. 4 sec.)

The husband offers his wife Joan a duckling that sings "Good Morning to You." The husband and wife go out together. Tom returns through the chimney and sees the duckling. He swallows him, but the duckling escapes through Tom's ear, which he has opened like a window. He hides in Jerry's bed. Tom captures the duckling, but Jerry trips Tom up, and the duckling escapes. The

Note
• This film marks the last appearance of the duckling, who had become one of Tom and Jerry's regular partners.

duckling covers himself with cold cream and becomes invisible; he hits Tom, who has been threatening Jerry. Jerry makes himself invisible and Tom sees a number of surprising things begin to happen. The door opens all by itself, a watermelon is eaten, and someone puts a lot of pills on his tongue. He can't understand what is going on. Jerry and the duckling make Tom's tail invisible and take a false tail for a walk. They hit Tom and pinch him, and he's soon thrown out through the maildrop.

Jerry and the duckling take off the cream and reappear. Seeing them, Tom now understands what has been going on. He makes himself invisible and pursues Jerry and the duckling, striking at them with a coal shovel.

ROBIN HOODWINKED

Directors: William Hanna,
Joseph Barbera
Producers: William Hanna, Joseph
Barbera (Metro-Goldwyn-Mayer)
Animation: Kenneth Muse, Carlo
Vinci, Lewis Marshall, James Escalante
Music: Scott Bradley
Set Design: Robert Gentle
Tracing: Dick Bickenbach
Technicolor. CinemaScope (6 min.
15 sec.)

The setting is Sherwood Forest. Robin
Hood, a prisoner in the sheriff's jail, is
going to be hanged at dawn. "Nothing can
help him, absolutely nothing," says the narrator. But Jerry and Tuffy are determined to
act. They sneak into the castle and locate
the cell door, but Tom the guard is there!
Tuffy hits him with the cell key; then the
two mice grab the key back again. Tom pursues them, takes back the key, and swallows
it. Tom makes the mice fall into a hole in
the floor.

Jerry and Tuffy return while Tom is
sleeping. Tuffy goes down inside Tom and
takes back the key, but the string to which
it was attached breaks, and Tom swallows
both Tuffy and the precious key in one gulp.
Tom drinks some wine, and Tuffy soon gets
out through the mouth of the tipsy Tom.

Jerry knocks Tom out with a club. Tom
is "tonsured" with a hatchet. Robin Hood
succeeds in escaping, thanks to the key.
Tuffy is carried off by an arrow, shot by
Tom. Jerry starts running: He's carrying
both the arrow and Tuffy.

Note

• **Tuffy (Nibbles) appears for the thirteenth and last
time, twelve years after his arrival in "The Milky Waif."**

1958

TOT WATCHERS

Directors: William Hanna,
Joseph Barbera
Producers: William Hanna, Joseph
Barbera (Metro-Goldwyn-Mayer)
Animation: Lewis Marshall, James
Escalante, Kenneth Muse
Story: Homer Brightman
Music: Scott Bradley
Set Design: Robert Gentle
Tracing: Dick Bickenbach
Technicolor. CinemaScope (6 min.
28 sec.)

The mistress of the house goes out to do some errands, leaving her baby with the babysitter, Jeannie. Jeannie immediately gets on the telephone. Jerry, running away from Tom, hides in the baby's carriage. Tom arrives but Jeannie chases him away. The baby runs away from the carriage. Tom puts him back, but Jeannie hits Tom, thinking he's disturbing the baby.

Tom captures Jerry, but sees the baby, still gallivanting about, crawling into the dog kennel. He rushes over, but instead of carrying away the baby in his arms, he takes a dog. He nevertheless brings back the baby at last, and Jeannie goes at him again, with a broom. The baby leaves the house, falls onto a truck, and soon lands in a construction site. Tom rushes over. He stands between two metal beams in order to block the baby's fall. The baby passes from one beam to another. He falls. Tom catches him. The baby falls again. Tom and Jerry land in a casting of cement. The baby beats Tom on the head.

Tom and Jerry, exhausted, take the baby home. They are met by the police, who have been called in by Jeannie. They take Tom and Jerry away. The cop refuses to believe their story, but he suddenly sees the baby disappearing down the street.

Notes

- **Musical score: "Love That Pup" (Bradley).**

- **In this film, the baby, the couple, and Jeannie, the carefree babysitter, reappear. Spike makes only a brief appearance.**

- **This is the 114th and last film of the series begun eighteen years before. Without William Hanna and Joseph Barbera, Tom and Jerry will, sadly, never be the same again.**

Switchin' Kitten

Director: Gene Deitch
Producer: William L. Snyder
(Metro-Goldwyn-Mayer)
Story: Eli Bauer, Gene Deitch
Animation: Lu Guarnier, Gary Mooney
Metrocolor (8 min. 40 sec.)

The night is stormy. A cart drives up and a gleaming paw tosses out a package containing Tom. Inside the nearby castle, Jerry is working with a scientist on a mysterious experiment. He picks out the cat who has been chosen for the experiment. The cat is tied up next to a dog. The machine is switched on; the cat becomes a dog—or at least behaves like one—and vice versa. Tom arrives at the castle and grabs Jerry, who calls for the dog-cat, who hits Tom over the head. Jerry thanks him. Tom catches Jerry again, but the dog-cat begins to snarl and growl. Jerry throws him a bone. Tom tries, without success, to explain to the dog-cat that he, too, is a cat. The dog-cat flattens Tom between the pages of a book filled with photographs of cats. Tom runs after Jerry. The dog-cat hits him, and Tom is shot outside. He then finds himself inside the circuit set up by Jerry and the scientist. Tom manages to escape. He sees a whistling elephant, a rooster who acts like a sheep, and a meowing dog. Overcome, he begs for mercy from Jerry, who begins roaring like a lion and soon nestles in the famous Metro-Goldwyn-Mayer logo. Tom shoots away like a rocket.

Note
• This is the first film of the series directed by Gene Deitch.

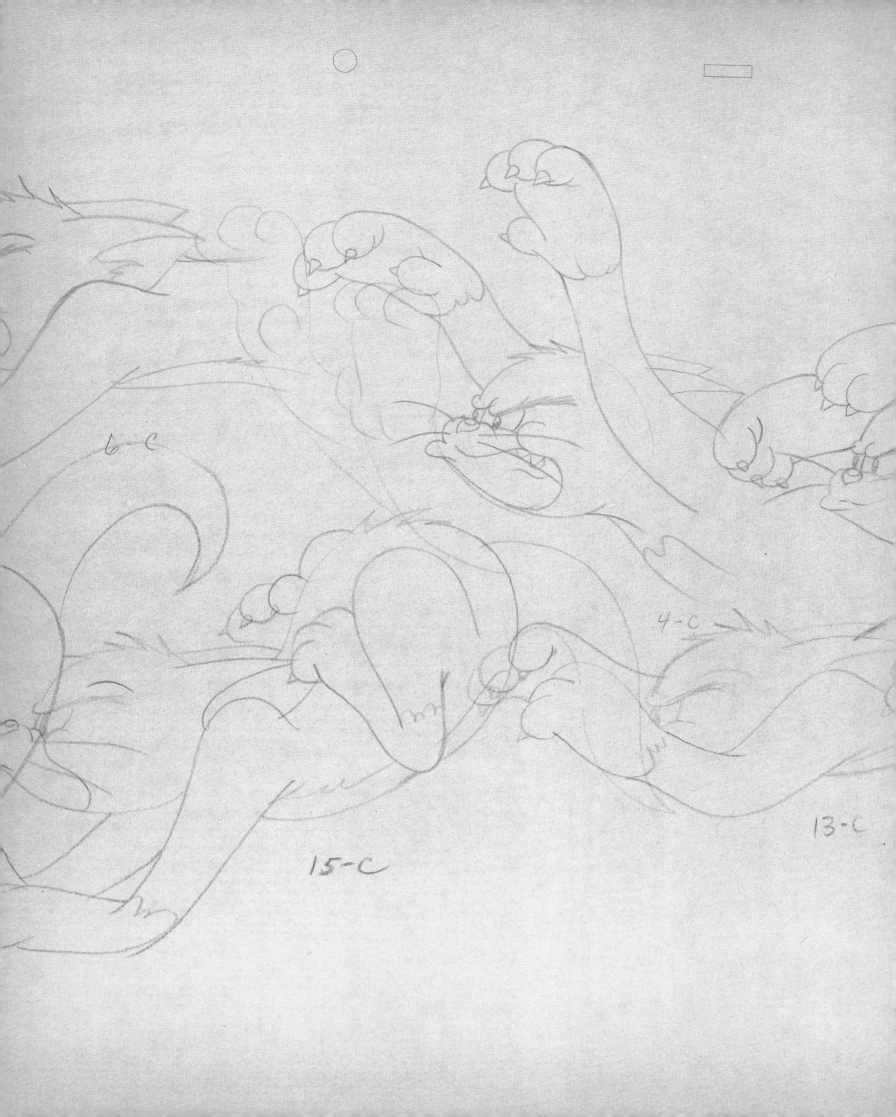

1961

DOWN AND OUTING

Director: Gene Deitch
Producer: William L. Snyder
(Metro-Goldwyn-Mayer)
Story: Larz Bourne
Animation: no credits given
Sound Effects: Tod Dockstader
Voice: Allen Swift
Technicolor (6 min. 49 sec.)

Tom wakes up and prepares to go fishing with his master. Jerry goes with them. The car leaves, first without Jerry, then without Tom. The cat catches up with the vehicle. While trying to hit Jerry, he strikes the driver. Jerry steps on the accelerator. The driver crushes Tom's paw, and Tom falls out on the road. He puts out a fire in his rear end in a nearby pond, which immediately dries up. The driver attaches Tom to the seat, but Jerry draws a mouse on the driver's foot, who soon beats up Tom. The driver catches Tom with his fishing rod. A fishing party begins on board the "Sea Note." Tom throws Jerry in the water, but the mouse gets back at him by attaching the hook on Tom's rod to the driver. As the film ends, Jerry and the fisherman are quietly fishing away, while Tom is all tied up in a basket, with a fish landing, from time to time, on his head.

1961

IT'S GREEK TO ME-OW!

Director: Gene Deitch
Producer: William L. Snyder
(Metro-Goldwyn-Mayer)
Story: Eli Bauer
Animation: no credits given
Sound Effects: Tod Dockstader
Voice: Allen Swift
Technicolor (6 min. 46 sec.)

The setting is Athens. Tom is looking for food. He sees Jerry eating in a relaxed position. He extends his arm and soon gets it back right in the face, with a smack. He launches a bullet with a catapult, and it falls on his paw. Chased by a guard, he traps Jerry in a bottle, but can't get him out. Tom is hit on the head by a vase, and then by a column,

thrown by Jerry. Pushed into a trash can, he reappears, looking like a monster. Jerry, now in soldier's garb, flattens his tail with a rock and knocks him out with a club. Tom lands in a chariot from which the horses soon disappear. Jerry hurls it into the abyss. Tom runs away screaming.

"Ah, yes," says the narrator, "the Greeks have a word for it!"

HIGH STEAKS

Director: Gene Deitch
Producer: William L. Snyder
(Metro-Goldwyn-Mayer)
Director of Animation:
Vaclav Bedrich
Story: Larz Bourne
Voices: Allen Swift
Technicolor (6 min. 21 sec.)

A man is preparing a barbecue. Tom is on the scene when Jerry comes along. Tom grabs him and throws him out. Tom and Jerry then duel with forks, and Tom accidentally sticks the man in the rear. Jerry

hides in a badminton shuttlecock. Tom hits it with a racket and sends the shuttlecock flying so that it lands in the man's mouth. He strikes Tom. Jerry spills some Kooky Kola on the barbecue meat. The man holds Tom responsible and makes him drink the contents of the bottle. Jerry laughs and then dips Tom's tail into the barbecue. Tom runs away, screaming. He dives into the pool, and the man fishes him out and ties him up. Jerry then transports Tom into the street and attaches him to a car that carries him off into the distance. Jerry, now rid of Tom, greedily devours a steak.

MOUSE INTO SPACE

Director: Gene Deitch
Producer: William L. Snyder
(Metro-Goldwyn-Mayer)
Director of Animation:
Vaclav Bedrich
Story: Tod Dockstader
Technicolor (6 min. 34 sec.)

Jerry, fed up with Tom's harassment, decides to become a mouse astronaut and go off into space, where there are no cats. He packs his valise. Tom sees him leaving and tries to keep him from going by shooting him, striking him, and blowing him up with a bomb. Jerry goes to the astronauts' training center, takes a series of tests, and is declared fit for service. Meanwhile, Tom has become an alcoholic tramp. He hides in a pipe and soon finds himself being shot into space on a rocket. Tom gets into the cabin and harasses Jerry, who's inside. Tom is ejected and reaches another spaceship whose astronaut is a Soviet dog! Tom is hit by a shower of meteorites and falls through space, landing on the ground after a dizzying descent. There he finds Jerry, proudly sporting an astronaut's license. Tom sets it on fire. Jerry starts to chase him, and Tom takes to his heels.

LANDING STRIPLING

Director: Gene Deitch
Producer: William L. Snyder
(Metro-Goldwyn-Mayer)
Director of Animation:
Vaclav Bedrich
Story: Eli Bauer
Technicolor (6 min. 18 sec.)

Tom is asleep. He is awakened by a bird, whom he captures and strikes. Jerry appears and saws away at a pole. When it falls Tom is thrown into a pot of boiling water. The unhappy cat loses some of his fur. He tries flooding Jerry's mouse hole with water, and soon finds himself caught in the water hose. He disguises himself as a birdman, but Jerry sends him off with the help of a ventilator. Tom fires a cannon, but Jerry has placed Tom's tail in the cannonball and Tom is thrown into a tree. He surveys the terrain with ground-lights, hoping to attract the bird, but he is soon carried off by a real

airplane. The plane goes into a dive and lands Tom in the bird's tree. The bird pastes an airmail sticker on Tom's head.

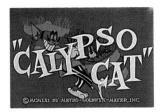

CALYPSO CAT

Director: Gene Deitch
Producer: William L. Snyder
(Metro-Goldwyn-Mayer)
Director of Animation:
Vaclav Bedrich
Music: Steven Konichek
Story: Larz Bourne
Technicolor (7 min. 59 sec.)

Tom is chasing Jerry. Jerry hides in a sack. Tom falls into some water. He manages to embed Jerry in aspic. Chasing him once more, he suddenly notices a seductive white kitten. He forgets about Jerry, who tries to attract his attention by setting fire to his paw. The white kitten boards the Caribbean Queen. Tom and Jerry also manage to board the ship. Tom offers the kitten some pastry, but Jerry intervenes and the kitten is spattered with cake. Tom tries to clean her up, but bruises her. The kitten hits him with a tray. Tom offers her some flowers, but she gets soaked by the water from a tube under the bouquet. The Caribbean Queen finally docks, and the white kitten, simpering, disembarks with Tom. She turns her attention to a calypso musician with whom Tom has a fight. Lamenting the loss of his ladylove, he consoles himself by chasing Jerry all through the return trip. Tom and Jerry meet up back where they started.

DICKY MOE

Director: Gene Deitch
Producer: William L. Snyder
(Metro-Goldwyn-Mayer)
Animation: Vaclav Bedrich
Music: Steven Konichek
Story: Eli Bauer and Gene Deitch
Voices: Allen Swift
Technicolor (7 min. 5 sec.)

A mad, one-legged sea captain tells of his obsession: Dicky Moe, the white whale. Frightened, the crew quits the ship, the Kumquat. The captain knocks out Tom and kidnaps him. Tom awakens on the Kumquat. He's hoping for a rest but the captain makes

him scrub the deck. Jerry, meanwhile, is quietly reading. Tom scrubs him almost to the point of transparency. Jerry replaces the water Tom's been using with black grease, which then dirties rather than cleans. Jerry laughs. Tom is hit on the head by the bucket of grease and turns completely black. He eludes the captain's rage by pretending to be his shadow. He tries flattening Jerry with an anvil but gets smashed himself. The captain sights Dicky Moe. He fires at the beast with his harpoon cannon and Tom, who has been holding the end of the cord, is suddenly propelled forward and finds himself tied to the side of Dicky Moe, who carries him off into the distance.

Note
• The theme is obviously an allusion to *Moby Dick*.

1962

THE TOM AND JERRY CARTOON KIT

Director: Gene Deitch
Producer: William L. Snyder
(Metro-Goldwyn-Mayer)
Director of Animation:
Vaclav Bedrich
Music: Steven Konichek
Story: Chris Jenkyns
Voices: Allen Swift
Technicolor (6 min. 28 sec.)

A kit contains Tom and Jerry figures. The mouse emerges and eats a watermelon. Then Tom comes out and flicks Jerry with his finger. Jerry dances. Tom puts him in a box and begins to dance himself. Tom finishes the watermelon and, with his mouth

serving as a kind of cannon, shoots the seeds at Jerry.

Jerry emerges from a book on judo and Tom goes to the mat. The cat practices boxing; he tries landing a blow on Jerry, but the mouse sends him reeling. He tries attacking him with a combat weapon, but gets all tangled up. Tom enters judo class and gets a diploma. Jerry breaks a stone. Tom goes to work on an enormous block and gets swallowed up in the ground. Jerry then shuts him up in the box labeled "The End."

1962

TALL IN THE TRAP

Director: Gene Deitch
Producer: William L. Snyder
(Metro-Goldwyn-Mayer)
Story: Bill Danch, Ted Pierce,
Gene Deitch
Music: Steven Konichek
Voices: Allen Swift
Metrocolor (7 min. 49 sec.)

D ry Gulch, a small western town, has a particularly ineffectual sheriff. Mutt Dillin is unable to lay a hand on Jerry, wanted for cheese robbery. He calls in a specialist, Tom, and asks him to capture Jerry. Tom and Jerry face it out in the town's main street, but Tom loses his pants while drawing his gun. He chases Jerry, who takes shelter in a saloon. Jerry knocks out Tom. Tom pursues the mouse and falls down the stairs. Jerry shoots Tom with the cat's own gun. The chase begins again. Tom draws on a mousetrap and a piece of cheese, but it's Tom who gets caught. He prepares a trap with gunpowder and is blown up. Mutt Dillin, the sheriff, chases after him with his gun while Jerry grabs another piece of cheese.

Note

- The sheriff's name, Mutt Dillin, is an allusion to Matt Dillon, the character played by James Arness in the television series "Gunsmoke."

1962

SORRY SAFARI

Director: Gene Deitch
Producer: William L. Snyder
(Metro-Goldwyn-Mayer)
Story: Larz Bourne
Music: Steven Konichek
Voices: Allen Swift
Metrocolor (7 min. 17 sec.)

A hunter arrives at the Nairobi airport. Out of his valise comes Tom and out of a hatbox comes Jerry. The hunter leaves on safari on an elephant's back. Tom soon ends up in a tree. The hunter ties a knot around Tom with his gun. The elephant crushes Tom. The hunter falls off his elephant, and he's growing very angry. A lion appears. He attacks the hunter, whose gun Tom has replaced with a thermos bottle. The hunter remounts the elephant, who crushes Tom's paws. Tom shakes Jerry. A rhinoceros arrives. The elephant, seeing Jerry, is frightened. The rhinoceros chases the hunter, Tom, and Jerry. He is hit by a tree branch. As the film ends, Jerry and the elephant are carrying the rhinoceros, the hunter, and Tom, like the spoils of a fruitful hunt.

1962

BUDDIES THICKER THAN WATER

Director: Gene Deitch
Producer: William L. Snyder
(Metro-Goldwyn-Mayer)
Story: Larz Bourne
Music: Steven Konichek
Technicolor (8 min. 58 sec.)

New York is covered with snow. Jerry is relaxing in a luxurious apartment while, outside in the blizzard, Tom is freezing to death. Jerry receives a message of distress from Tom: "Help! I'm freezing!" Signed, "Your old pal, Tom." And then another message: "I'm dying of hunger, too. Tom." Jerry goes to the aid of Tom, who is completely frozen. He warms him with an electric blanket, feeds him, and soon they're tossing off a bottle of champagne. But the mistress of the house arrives and wants to throw Tom out. The cat shows Jerry to her; she screams, and Tom chases Jerry out of the house. The woman strokes him. Jerry covers himself in powder, puts on a record, dims the light and appears like a ghost. Tom is terrified. He then discovers the truth but falls into the snow. He sends Jerry a new distress signal. Jerry responds by sending him a hockey player's outfit.

1962

CARMEN GET IT!

Director: Gene Deitch
Producer: William L. Snyder
(Metro-Goldwyn-Mayer)
Story: Gene Deitch
Music played by the Tom and Jerry Symphony Orchestra (100 Men and a Mouse) directed by Steven Konichek
Technicolor (7 min. 38 sec.)

Tom chases Jerry along Broadway. They find themselves in front of the Metropolitan Opera. The usher chases Tom away, but he manages to sneak in, hidden behind a cello. Tom sits down in the orchestra and plays a violin, inside of which a miniature tape player plays the music of *Carmen*. Tom rubs his bow with a piece of cheese and strikes Jerry with the bow. Jerry plays the tape player in reverse and the conductor, furious, breaks the violin over Tom's head. Jerry hides in the conductor's suit, so that he begins jigging about in the middle of the overture to *Carmen*. The conductor traps Tom between the pages of the score and

continues to direct. Jerry discovers some ants and, by playing the flute, attracts them toward the score. Under the blare of the lights, Tom conducts the *Carmen* overture, but the ants begin to move and the score moves with them. Tom grabs Jerry, screws him in like an electric bulb, and turns the switch on. The conductor returns. The singer playing Carmen sees Jerry and runs away. Tom finds himself facing the conductor like a toreador confronting a maddened bull. They chase after one another while Jerry leads the orchestra in a brilliant rendition of the music.

Note
• This is the last of the thirteen films directed by Gene Deitch.

1963

PENT-HOUSE MOUSE

Director: Chuck Jones
Producer: Chuck Jones
(Metro-Goldwyn-Mayer)
Production Supervisor: Les Goldman
Codirector: Maurice Noble
Animation: Ken Harris, Tom Ray, Dick Thompson, Ben Washam
Story: Chuck Jones, Michael Maltese
Music: Eugene Poddany
Set Design: Philip Deguard
Vocal Effects: Mel Blanc
Executive Director: Walter Bien
Metrocolor (7 min. 8 sec.)

Tom is lolling about on a luxurious terrace, living the life of Riley. Outside, Jerry is hungry, very hungry. He falls from a skyscraper construction site in which he's been hiding out. Tom catches him, but Jerry finds he's landed on a slice of bread in Tom's paw. Tom chases after him. Jerry enters Tom's head through his mouth, closing the cat's ears and then his eyes. Tom chases him and gets hit with a shovel. Tom falls through space, then rolls away on a barrel, just managing to avoid danger, and ends up in a dog show. Screams are heard. Jerry is lolling about on the terrace. He swallows, through a straw, a large ice cube, soon assuming its shape.

Note
• This is the first film in the series produced and directed by Chuck Jones.

1 9 6 4

THE CAT ABOVE AND THE MOUSE BELOW

Director: Chuck Jones
Producer: Chuck Jones (A Sib-Tower 12 Production—Metro-Goldwyn-Mayer)
Production Supervisor: Les Goldman
Codirector: Maurice Noble
Animation: Tom Ray, Dick Thompson, Ben Washam, Ken Harris, Don Towsley
Story: Michael Maltese, Chuck Jones
Music: Eugene Poddany
Set Design: Philip Deguard
Baritone: Terence Monck
Metrocolor (6 min. 27 sec.)

The famous baritone Signor Thomasino Catti-Cazzaza (that's Tom) arrives in a deluxe car, eludes his many admirers, goes on stage, and begins singing *Rigoletto*. The sound wakens Jerry, who has been sleeping in his home below stage. He is soon fed up and taps on the ceiling to make it stop. He ties Tom's face with an elastic, but the cat responds by nailing him to the wall. Jerry tries to disturb Tom by licking a lemon during his singing. Tom takes revenge by pressing the lemon over Jerry's head. The mouse undoes Tom's shirtfront with a hook, then throws a glass at him. Tom throws Jerry against the wall, but one of the sacks of sand securing the stage setting falls down and sends Tom through the floor. Jerry then takes Tom's place and sings to the applause of the audience while Tom, from below, raps on the ceiling.

1 9 6 4

IS THERE A DOCTOR IN THE MOUSE?

Director: Chuck Jones
Producer: Chuck Jones (A Sib-Tower 12 Production—Metro-Goldwyn-Mayer)
Codirector: Maurice Noble
Production Supervisor: Les Goldman
Animation: Ben Washam, Ken Harris, Don Towsley, Tom Ray, Dick Thompson
Story: Michael Maltese, Chuck Jones
Set Design: Robert Gribbroek
Music: Eugene Poddany
Vocal Effects: Mel Blanc
Technicolor (7 min. 13 sec.)

Jerry prepares and then drinks a mysterious potion. Tom gets ready to eat a sardine. Jerry, who's acquired an amazing strength and swiftness, swoops down upon it and eats it before Tom can even see him. Five more sardines in the can meet the same fate. Tom imagines that a ghost or a jet-engined bee has arrived. Jerry devours the watermelon, the chicken, and then all the

fruit. Tom hides in the refrigerator. Jerry continues to eat away.

Tom has decided to discover who the thief is, and installs both a camera and a caketrap. He shoots the film, develops it, and discovers Jerry!

Tom places a mousetrap in a sandwich. Jerry arrives, devours the bread, and leaves the trap, which closes on Tom. But Jerry suddenly loses his strength and swiftness. He remixes his potion, drinks it, and begins to swell up.

Tom, who's been waiting in front of Jerry's mouse hole, draws him out by the tail and suddenly retrieves a giant mouse. He starts to laugh, and then to cry!

1 9 6 4

MUCH ADO ABOUT MOUSING

Director: Chuck Jones
Producer: Chuck Jones (Metro-Goldwyn-Mayer)
Executive Producer: Walter Bien
Production Supervisor: Les Goldman
Codirector: Maurice Noble
Animation: Ben Washam, Ken Harris, Don Towsley, Tom Ray, Dick Thompson
Music: Eugene Poddany
Story: Michael Maltese
Set Design: Philip Deguard
Vocal Effects: Mel Blanc
Metrocolor (6 min. 38 sec.)

On the docks, Tom is fishing for Jerry with some cheese. Chasing him, he crashes into a wall. Jerry hides between the jaws of a big dog. Tom pulls the dog's tongue to get Jerry out. The dog rolls Tom into a ball and throws him into the water. Tom is attacked by a crab. The dog, egged on by Tom, is hauled away by the dogcatcher. Jerry rescues him and the dog tells him, "Any time you need me, just whistle." Jerry whistles and Tom is thrown into the water. Tom puts some earmuffs on the dog, who can't hear a thing. Jerry whistles and shows Tom some earmuffs. Tom, thinking they're the ones belonging to the dog, jumps into the water. Jerry then dons earmuffs and settles down next to the dog.

1964

SNOWBODY LOVES ME

Director: Chuck Jones
Producer: Chuck Jones (A Sib-Tower
12 Production—Metro-Goldwyn-
Mayer)
Codirector: Maurice Noble
Production Supervisor: Les Goldman
Animation: Dick Thompson, Ben
Washam, Ken Harris, Don Towsley,
Tom Ray
Music: Eugene Poddany
Story: Michael Maltese, Chuck Jones
Set Design: Philip Deguard
Vocal Effects: Mel Blanc
Metrocolor (7 min. 48 sec.)

Jerry, frozen with cold, arrives in a small village. He discovers a house full of cheese. He knocks at the door, awakens Tom, and enters the house, leaving Tom suddenly outside. Tom sees Jerry making a fire. He tries to enter through the chimney, but soon finds himself ejected, outside once more.

Jerry is up to his ears in cheese. Tom lights a fire. Jerry, inside the cheese, sings a Tyrolean song. Tom fills the Swiss cheese holes with corks and the cheese finally explodes under the pressure of air from a big pair of bellows upon which an anvil has fallen. Tom is covered with corks and bits of cheese. Jerry, clad in a ballerina's skirt made of cheese, does a dance. Tom hits him and kicks him out, but soon, ashamed of his behavior, imagines the mouse turning into a ghost. He goes out to get him and revives him with some 90 proof Eulenspiegel cognac.

Jerry makes his appearance in Tyrolean costume and dances to Tom's accompaniment on the piano.

1964

THE UNSHRINKABLE JERRY MOUSE

Director: Chuck Jones
Producer: Chuck Jones (A Sib-Tower
12 Production—Metro-Goldwyn-
Mayer)
Codirector: Maurice Noble
Production Supervisor: Les Goldman
Animation: Dick Thompson, Ben
Washam, Ken Harris, Don Towsley,
Tom Ray
Music: Eugene Poddany
Story: Michael Maltese, Chuck Jones
Set Design: Philip Deguard
Vocal Effects: Mel Blanc
Metrocolor (6 min. 45 sec.)

Tom is a house cat and lives in splendid tranquillity. Jerry goes to fetch him his milk. But a delivery man brings a red-and-white-haired kitten to the house, and the blond, young mistress of the house pets it. Tom knows that having one cat around is heaven, but that two are hell. He wants to throw the kitten out, but Jerry arrives to save him. Tom begins again, and Jerry saves the kitten a second time. Tom is thrown out of the house. He tries to get back in and threatens Jerry, but in vain; the mouse won't let him in. He's upset at seeing Jerry feeding the little cat. He charges toward them, falls on a roller skate, slips on a banana peel, and ends up embedded in the door. He catches his head in a window while trying to enter. Jerry thrashes him from behind, and Tom ends up by pleading for peace. In the end, Tom is massaging Jerry while the kitten drinks his milk.

1965

AH, SWEET MOUSE-STORY OF LIFE

Director: Chuck Jones
Producer: Chuck Jones
(Metro-Goldwyn-Mayer)
Production Supervisor: Les Goldman
Codirector: Maurice Noble
Animation: Dick Thompson, Ben
Washam, Ken Harris, Don Towsley,
Tom Ray
Story: Michael Maltese, Chuck Jones
Music: Eugene Poddany
Set Design: Robert Gribbroek
Vocal Effects: June Foray, Mel Blanc
Metrocolor (6 min.)

Tom is chasing Jerry. He cuts out the wall around Jerry's mouse hole and soon finds himself flattened against it. Next, caught in some drapes, Tom is dangling in midair and so is Jerry. Jerry hooks onto a question mark, while Tom hooks onto an exclamation mark and falls onto the ground and into a sewer. Then, under the shock of an alarm, he loses his fur coat. Jerry conjures up a set of daggers and throws them at Tom. Tom chases after Jerry and is caught in a rainspout. Jerry manages (so to speak) to release him with the sound of the loud alarm. Tom thanks him. He is now all stretched out, which doesn't prevent him from continuing the chase after Jerry.

Note

• The idea of the question mark, the exclamation mark, and the daggers imagined by Jerry, then materialized, recall certain surprising gags from the Felix the Cat series.

1965

TOM-IC ENERGY

Director: Chuck Jones
Producer: Chuck Jones (A Sib-Tower 12 Production—Metro-Goldwyn-Mayer)
Production Supervisor: Les Goldman
Codirector: Maurice Noble
Animation: Ken Harris, Don Towsley, Tom Ray, Dick Thompson, Ben Washam
Story: Michael Maltese, Chuck Jones
Music: Eugene Poddany
Set Design: Philip Deguard
Vocal Effects: Mel Blanc
Metrocolor (6 min. 45 sec.)

Tom has scared Jerry to death. Jerry's ghost appears to Tom, who is immediately transformed into a pale old cat. Tom pursues Jerry upstairs from one story to the next, until they reach the sky. Tom, learning from Jerry that he is in the void, falls to the ground. Tom continues chasing Jerry in the street. They pass other cats chasing other mice. Tom falls into a manhole, then emerges, but is hit on the paw by the manhole cover. His paw is crushed. Jerry arrives

and blows it up again, but Tom, now grown bigger and bigger, soon rises into the air. Shot upward into the air, he arrives on a rooftop, where he is pursued by a tomcat who kisses him. The tomcat, knocked out by Tom, takes it philosophically.

Tom continues to chase Jerry. He runs into a big dog who starts to chase him. Jerry, displeased by this, transforms the dog into an accordion. Tom thanks Jerry and continues to pursue him.

1965

BAD DAY AT CAT ROCK

Director: Chuck Jones
Producer: Chuck Jones (Metro-Goldwyn-Mayer)
Production Supervisor: Les Goldman
Codirector: Maurice Noble
Animation: Ben Washam, Ken Harris, Don Towsley, Dick Thompson
Story: Chuck Jones
Music: Eugene Poddany
Set Design: Philip Deguard
Tracing: Erni Nordli
Metrocolor (6 min. 15 sec.)

Tom and Jerry are chasing each other on a scaffolding. Tom falls down a sewer. He lights a match, which illuminates the credits list, then ignites some TNT. Explosion. Tom in embedded in a metal girder. Jerry falls, using Tom's fur as a parachute. Tom "dresses" again. Jerry crawls into a glove and strikes Tom, who falls beneath the weight of a beam. He goes after Jerry. They go looking for one another. Tom, trying to stick Jerry in the behind, sticks himself. Tom tries to catch up with Jerry by using a beam and a weight, but fails each time. Jerry then peacefully paints "The End."

Note

• The title is an allusion to John Sturges' film *Bad Day at Black Rock*, with Spencer Tracy and Robert Ryan.

1965

THE BROTHERS CARRY-MOUSE-OFF

Director: Jim Pabian
Producer: Chuck Jones (Metro-Goldwyn-Mayer)
Production Supervisor: Les Goldman
Codirector: Maurice Noble
Animation: Tom Ray, Dick Thompson, Ben Washam, Ken Harris, Don Towsley
Story: Chuck Jones, Jim Pabian
Production Director: Earl Jonas
Music: Eugene Poddany
Set Design: Robert Gribbroek
Metrocolor (6 min. 27 sec.)

Jerry is resting beside a swimming pool when his radar warns him of Tom's arrival. He hides. Tom puts out food to attract Jerry, but the mouse easily grabs it. Tom finally catches Jerry, who hits him with a little mallet, which has suddenly grown huge. He uses the flattened Tom as a doormat. Tom tries to blow himself up again with a bellows, but it's Jerry who works the bellows, and Tom soon lands in a fish bowl. He gets out, takes a fish out of his mouth, and chases after Jerry. The mouse opens a door, which leads to fall through the air. Tom dresses up as a mouse and plays a ukelele. His perfume attracts a swarm of mice who rush toward him. Tom runs off; unable to shed his mouse costume, he finds himself being pursued by a band of vengeful cats.

HAUNTED MOUSE

Director: Chuck Jones
Producer: Chuck Jones
(Metro-Goldwyn-Mayer)
Production Supervisor: Les Goldman
Codirector: Maurice Noble
Animation: Ben Washam, Ken Harris,
Don Towsley, Tom Ray, Dick
Thompson
Story: Jim Pabian, Chuck Jones
Music: Eugene Poddany
Set Design: Philip Deguard
Vocal Effects: Mel Blanc
Metrocolor (6 min. 49 sec.)

Jerry, possessed of magical powers, appears. He lifts Tom—thanks to magic—and goes to meet his girlfriend. His clothes arrange themselves on the hanger all by themselves. The girlfriend takes an elevator to the refrigerator. She takes a radish, then plucks the end of Tom's nose. Tom replaces the tip of his nose with a radish. Tom chases her and catches Jerry, but Jerry manages to hypnotize Tom. Jerry seizes the opportunity to enter Tom's mouth and descend into his body. He opens various doors and we see several mice and birds, as well as a fish, emerging from Tom's mouth. The cat is knocked out by an ironing board. He's frightened by Jerry, but realizes that the mouse confronting him is not the dangerous mouse in question. Tom takes three rabbits out of Jerry's hat. They knock him cold with a mallet. Beaten, Tom surrenders, and Jerry leaves, after having materialized the word "End."

I'M JUST WILD ABOUT JERRY

Director: Chuck Jones
Producer: Chuck Jones
(Metro-Goldwyn-Mayer)
Production Supervisor: Les Goldman
Codirector: Maurice Noble
Animation: Dick Thompson, Ben
Washam, Ken Harris, Don Towsley
Story: Michael Maltese, Chuck Jones
Music: Eugene Poddany
Set Design: Philip Deguard
Metrocolor (6 min. 39 sec.)

Tom is in pursuit of Jerry. He soon finds himself on a railway track, where he twice just misses getting run over by a train. He starts to chase after Jerry again, but his tail gets stuck in a mailbox and stretches to an abnormal length. Jerry arrives on a fire engine. Tom climbs up and takes over command of the car. He chases Jerry, but is struck by a bowling ball. Jerry takes cover in a crowd of toy mice who look like him. Tom finds him and plays Ping-Pong, using Jerry as the ball. Jerry knocks him out with a croquet mallet and sends him reeling out of the house. Tom lands on the railway track, but is not run over by a train: Jerry—the angel—has maneuvered the signal switches.

OF FELINE BONDAGE

Director: Chuck Jones
Producer: Chuck Jones
(Metro-Goldwyn-Mayer)
Production Supervisor: Les Goldman
Codirector: Maurice Noble
Animation: Ben Washam, Don Towsley,
Ken Harris, Tom Ray, Dick Thompson
Story: Don Towsley, Chuck Jones
Music: Eugene Poddany
Set Design: Robert Gribbroek
Vocal Effects: June Foray, Mel Blanc
Metrocolor (6 min. 35 sec.)

Tom captures Jerry in a box and sends him rolling, like dice. He throws him onto a billiard table, where Jerry is squashed by the eight ball. A mouse-fairy now appears. Jerry explains his problem. The fairy is shocked. She gives Jerry a vial. He drinks the contents and becomes invisible. He grabs the cheese with which Tom has tried to trap him. He ties up Tom's nose, drags him along, and almost cuts off his tail. Tom is terrified. Jerry cuts off his whiskers and shaves his skull. Tom is soon in tatters. He takes his revenge, and Jerry is half undressed, as if he were wearing a fur swim suit.

Both Tom and Jerry break into laughter, rolling about in glee.

THE YEAR OF THE MOUSE

Director: Chuck Jones
Producer: Chuck Jones
(Metro-Goldwyn-Mayer)
Production Supervisor: Les Goldman
Codirector: Maurice Noble
Animation: Dick Thompson, Ben Washam, Ken Harris, Don Towsley
Story: Michael Maltese, Chuck Jones
Music: Eugene Poddany
Set Design: Philip Deguard
Vocal Effects: June Foray, Mel Blanc
Metrocolor (7 min. 23 sec.)

Tom is resting by the fireside. Jerry, with the help of a gray mouse, comes down through the chimney, hits Tom, and disappears. Tom can't figure out what's happening! Jerry fires a revolver at Tom and disappears. Tom finds himself holding the revolver. He still can't understand. Tom tugs at a cord knotted around his neck and almost hangs himself. He's hit on the head by the ceiling lamp. He finds a knife in his hand and thinks he's killed himself. Finally, he begins to see what's really happening. Stretching himself, he's projected, like an arrow, by a bow placed there by Jerry. Tom finally catches the two mice and shuts them up in a bottle, threatening them with a revolver. Finally, he can relax and fan himself.

Note
- The film's first title was "Tom Thumb."

THE CAT'S ME-OUCH

Director: Chuck Jones
Producer: Chuck Jones
(Metro-Goldwyn-Mayer)
Production Supervisor: Les Goldman
Codirector: Maurice Noble
Animation: Don Towsley, Tom Ray, Dick Thompson, Ben Washam, Ken Harris
Story: Michael Maltese, Chuck Jones
Music: Eugene Poddany
Set Design: Philip Deguard
Vocal Effects: June Foray, Mel Blanc
Metrocolor (6 min. 14 sec.)

Tom pursues Jerry with an ax. Jerry sees a magazine ad announcing a dog for sale and imagines a mastiff chasing Tom. He writes a letter and mails it. He's already laughing at the idea of what's going to happen. A truck delivers an enormous case, out of which jumps a very affectionate little dog. Tom slyly bounces the puppy in his paw, but the dog devours both paws and turns Tom's tail into a string of sausages. Tom runs away and Jerry congratulates his new ally. But Tom catches Jerry and puts him in a jar. The dog attacks, and Tom is thrown out of the house. Tom returns, armed with an ax, and breaks down the door. The dog eats the handle and Tom is injured. Tom is now in the hospital. The dog is still hanging on to his foot while Jerry holds his tail.

JERRY-GO-ROUND

Director: Abe Levitow
Producer: Chuck Jones
(Metro-Goldwyn-Mayer)
Director of Production: Les Goldman
Animation: Dick Thompson, Ben Washam, Ken Harris, Don Towsley, Tom Ray
Story: John Dunn
Music: Eugene Poddany
Set Design: Philip Deguard
Tracing: Don Morgan
Graphics Advisor: Maurice Noble
Metrocolor (6 min. 22 sec.)

Tom is chasing Jerry, who hides in a circus. He sees an elephant who's crying over a nail stuck in his foot. Jerry removes it. The elephant strikes out at Tom. He's glad the pain is gone and is grateful to Jerry. Tom climbs a ladder to go after Jerry. The elephant smacks him. In the ring, Jerry, dressed as a clown, dances. He and the elephant play with a balloon. Tom pops the balloon and

grabs Jerry, who is balancing on a high wire. The elephant rescues Jerry and sends Tom flying out through the top of the tent.

Jerry jumps into a basin of water. The elephant empties the basin, and when Tom jumps, he is buried in the ground. A devil brings him back up to the surface. The elephant plays with Jerry, but Tom blows pepper in his face, and Jerry is sent flying. The elephant catches him and brings him back.

It's time for the parade. Tom tries to blow up Jerry and the elephant with dynamite, but he's the one who is blown up instead.

DUEL PERSONALITY

Director: Chuck Jones
Producer: Chuck Jones
(Metro-Goldwyn-Mayer)
Codirector: Maurice Noble
Production Supervisor: Les Goldman
Story: Chuck Jones, Michael Maltese
Animation: Don Towsley, Tom Ray,
Dick Thompson, Ben Washam, Ken
Harris
Music: Dean Elliott
Production Director: Earl Jonas
Set Design: Philip Deguard
Vocal Effects: June Foray
Metrocolor (6 min. 9 sec.)

The scene is a big castle. Tom is chasing Jerry with a bowling ball. Jerry strikes him with a glove. Tom and Jerry prepare for the duel.

The action shifts to the dueling ground. Tom and Jerry face off with pistols. They hit one another. Then they fight with swords and hit each other again. Next comes a duel with bow and arrow. Each of the two adversaries is sent flying and they collide. They confront each other in a duel by cannon. The two cannonballs collide and send the cannons flying into the distance. Tom and Jerry next fight with catapults and collide with each other. Tom begins chasing Jerry again with a bowling ball. Jerry—once again —tries to slap him, but it's Tom who slaps Jerry, striking him with the glove!

JERRY, JERRY, QUITE CONTRARY

Director: Chuck Jones
Producer: Chuck Jones
(Metro-Goldwyn-Mayer)
Production Supervisor: Les Goldman
Codirector: Maurice Noble
Animation: Ken Harris, Don Towsley,
Tom Ray, Dick Thompson,
Ben Washam, Al Pabian
Story: Chuck Jones
Director of Production: Earl Jonas
Music: Dean Elliott
Set Design: Philip Deguard
Vocal Effects: Mel Blanc
Metrocolor (7 min. 17 sec.)

Tom is sleeping. Jerry, walking in his sleep, comes out of his hole and pulls out two of Tom's whiskers. The cat shoots him into his hole with a billiard cue. Jerry "opens" Tom's tail like an umbrella and goes back into his hole. Tom spins Jerry about like a top. Jerry drinks coffee to stay awake, but falls asleep. He throws a brick at Tom, who locks him up in his hole. Jerry comes out, ties Tom's tail to an anvil, and throws him down into the chimney from the roof. Tom, overwhelmed by gravity, falls down through the house at a dizzy pace. Exhausted, he packs his valise and leaves for the desert. Jerry, still sleepwalking, follows him.

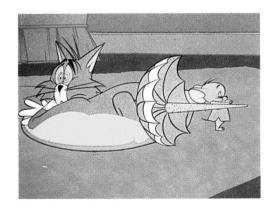

LOVE ME, LOVE MY MOUSE

Director: Chuck Jones, Ben Washam
Producer: Chuck Jones
(Metro-Goldwyn-Mayer)
Production Supervisor: Les Goldman
Animation: Ben Washam,
Philip Roman, Don Towsley,
Dick Thompson
Story: Michael Maltese
Music: Eugene Poddany
Graphics Advisor: Maurice Noble
Set Design: Robert Inman
Tracing: Robert Givens
Metrocolor (6 min. 34 sec.)

Tom daydreams about hearts while contemplating the photograph of his lady-love. Flying among the hearts, he sees the object of his passion and offers her Jerry as a gift. Jerry trembles with fear, but she comforts and coddles him. Tom has given her

Jerry to eat, but indignant, she hits Tom and takes care of Jerry. Thinking that Tom has eaten Jerry, she strikes him. Jerry turns on a recordplayer and the cat refuses to believe in Tom's innocence, accusing him of wanting to eat Jerry again. Tom, thrown out of the house, grabs hold of Jerry intending to crush him, but the female cat appears and Tom gets crushed by a falling steel object. The cat takes care of Jerry, and chases him in order to finally eat him, while the battered Tom watches.

PUSS 'N' BOATS

Director: Abe Levitow
Producer: Chuck Jones
(Metro-Goldwyn-Mayer)
Production Supervisor: Les Goldman
Animation: Ben Washam, Ken Harris,
Don Towsley, Tom Ray,
Dick Thompson
Story: Bob Ogle
Music: Carl Brandt
Graphics Advisor: Maurice Noble
Set Design: Philip Deguard
Tracing: Don Morgan
Metrocolor (6 min. 39 sec.)

Jerry is awakened by the smell of cheese, which appears like the hand of temptation. He spies a case of cheese, with Tom standing guard on the quay, a club in his hand. Jerry disguises himself as an officer, but Tom unmasks him and throws him in the water. Jerry is chased by a shark. While saving his superior officer, who was about to fall in, Tom is also threatened by the

shark. Tom chases Jerry and gets stretched out into a long, thin line.

Jerry tries to drown Tom with the ship's fire hose, but when he turns on the water, Tom is propelled into the air. He passes an American astronaut. Tom stops up the hose and it explodes. Tom falls into the mouth of the shark, who has been prompted by Jerry. He lands in the stoke hole and his tail catches fire. Tom falls into the water and the shark chases him into the distance. Jerry salutes the officer and climbs aboard. He happily does a sailor's dance.

FILET MEOW

Director: Abe Levitow
Producer: Chuck Jones
(Metro-Goldwyn-Mayer)
Production Supervisor: Les Goldman
Story: Bob Ogle
Animation: Don Towsley, Tom Ray,
Dick Thompson, Ben Washam,
Ken Harris
Music: Dean Elliott
Production Director: Earl Jonas
Set Design: Philip Deguard
Tracing: Don Morgan, Robert Givens
Advisor for Drawings: Maurice Noble
Metrocolor (6 min. 15 sec.)

Tom has his eye on a fish swimming in a jar. Jerry turns up and pricks Tom, then puts the fish back in the jar. Tom, protected by a trash can shield and armed with a hatchet, runs after Jerry but slices up his own tail and, slipping on some grease, winds up outside the house. The street cleaners empty him into a garbage truck. Tom returns, but Jerry is standing guard over the jar.

Tom makes a hole in the jar. Jerry holds back the fish while Tom sucks the water from the jar. Jerry lets a shark into the bathtub. Tom tries to swallow him. The shark chases Tom who flees the house, digging a trench as he goes. Jerry flees as well. The shark then joins the fish in the jar.

MATINEE MOUSE

Story, Direction, and Supervision:
Tom Ray
Producer: Metro-Goldwyn-Mayer
Animation: Ken Muse, Ed Barge, Irven
Spence, Ray Patterson, Lewis Marshall
Directors: William Hanna,
Joseph Barbera
Music: Dean Elliott
Additional Set Design: Philip Deguard
Sound Editing: Lovell Norman
Metrocolor (6 min. 7 sec.)

Tom is after Jerry. He's knocked out by a rake, a shovel, and various tools (sequence from "Love That Pup," 1949).

Trying to reach a canary, he lands on a perch but does not succeed (sequence from "The Flying Cat," 1952). He immobilizes Jerry between two pies. First Jerry, then Tom, is hit. They surrender with a white flag. Tom and Jerry walk down the street and go to a movie.

In the film, Spike follows a steak attached to a laundry line. Jerry tries vainly to warn him (sequence from "Love That Pup," 1949). Tom laughs at the situation. Jerry knocks his chair out from under him.

Tom mounts a witch's broom, does a balancing act, and ends up stuck in a tree while in midflight (sequence from "The Flying Sorceress," 1956).

Jerry laughs, but Tom takes his revenge. Tom hits Jerry with a pie, which spatters against the wall. Jerry can't understand this sudden anger (sequence from "Jerry's Diary," 1949).

Jerry, now angry, propels Tom up to the ceiling. Tom, still on his broom, flies over the cemetery and suddenly runs into the witch. He smashes into the ceiling and gets pasted into the table (sequence from "The Flying Sorceress," 1956). Jerry laughs, and this time Tom pulls the chair out from under him. From now on peace is impossible.

Spike, Tom, and Jerry, who have been fighting on the screen (sequence from "The Truce Hurts," 1948), stop and see Tom and Jerry fighting one another in the audience.

Note
• The film includes sequences from "Love That Pup" (1949), "The Flying Cat" (1952), "The Flying Sorceress" (1956), "Jerry's Diary" (1949), and "The Truce Hurts" (1948).

1966

THE A-TOM-INABLE SNOWMAN

Director: Abe Levitow
Producer: Chuck Jones
(Metro-Goldwyn-Mayer)
Production Supervisor: Les Goldman
Animation: Ken Harris, Don Towsley,
Tom Ray, Dick Thompson, Ben
Washam, Philip Roman
Story: Bob Ogle
Music: Dean Elliott
Production Direction: Earl Jonas
Set Design: Robert Inman
Tracing: Robert Givens
Advisor on Drawings: Maurice Noble
Metrocolor (6 min. 39 sec.)

Tom pours salt and pepper on Jerry, who sneezes his head off. Tom tries to eat him and swallows a bomb that explodes. Jerry runs away on skis. Tom chases after him. Jerry reaches a Red Cross shelter and snuggles up against a St. Bernard. Tom, in order to lure the dog away, pretends to be in danger. The dog comes out and Tom seizes the opportunity to pursue Jerry. Tom falls in the snow. Jerry informs the St. Bernard, who retrieves Tom in pieces. He revives him with the alcohol in his flask. Tom, now drunk, sees five Jerrys. He goes after Jerry and falls into a hole in the middle of a glacier. The St. Bernard rescues him and makes him drink. A drunken Tom starts to skate. He catches cold but succeeds in capturing and running away with Jerry.

The scene changes to an isle in the South Seas. Tom is cooking Jerry, who runs away. Tom is hit on the head by a coconut. The St. Bernard—again!—gives him something to drink. Tom, drunk again, leaves, skipping over the water.

1966

CATTY CORNERED

Director: Abe Levitow
Producer: Chuck Jones
(Metro-Goldwyn-Mayer)
Production Supervisor: Les Goldman
Story: John Dunn
Animation: Tom Ray, Dick
Thompson, Ben Washam, Ken Harris,
Don Towsley
Music: Carl Brandt
Production Director: Earl Jonas
Set Design: Hal Ashmead
Tracing: Don Morgan
Advisor on drawing: Maurice Noble
Technicolor (6 min. 18 sec.)

Jerry sees a piece of cheese and wants it. Tom hits him. A yellow cat runs after Jerry, who pulls out one of Tom's whiskers. Tom hits the yellow cat, who knocks him out. Both cats try to catch Jerry. Tom draws a bow and rips the yellow cat's fur apart. Tom gets pinned to the wall by a sword. The yellow cat shoots a catapult and the projectile is received and sent flying off by a cannon lying on a board. Tom counters with a cannon, and the yellow cat is hit by a cannonball that demolishes the wall he has been standing behind. Tom flings a stick of dynamite. Jerry returns it and the stick explodes right under Tom. The yellow cat and Tom each throw a grenade. Jerry watches them pass by, ending in a double explosion. The two cats leave the house and go off into the distance. Jerry runs after them.

1966

CAT AND DUPLI-CAT

Director: Chuck Jones
Producer: Chuck Jones
(Metro-Goldwyn-Mayer)
Production Supervisor: Les Goldman
Codirector: Maurice Noble
Animation: Dick Thompson, Ben
Washam, Ken Harris, Don Towsley,
Tom Ray
Story: Chuck Jones, Michael Maltese
Music: Eugene Poddany
Production Director: Earl Jonas
Set Design: Philip Deguard
Special Effects: Mel Blanc
Falsetto: Dale McKennon
Baritone: Terence Monck
Metrocolor (6 min. 45 sec.)

Tom, a real "poor man's" gondolier, sings "Santa Lucia." Jerry sings along. Tom grows furious and discovers the presence of a red cat. He sees Jerry in his rival's mouth. The rival cat pushes Tom into the water. Tom sends him flying and rescues Jerry. The second cat attaches Tom to a mast. Tom breaks loose, the rival cat sinks beneath the water, and Tom grabs Jerry. The red cat throws a bottle of champagne their way, and Jerry gets drunk. He ties the two cats together by their whiskers and leaves, singing, as the bubbles coming out of his mouth spell out "The End."

O-SOLAR MEOW

Director: Abe Levitow
Producer: Chuck Jones
(Metro-Goldwyn-Mayer)
Production Supervisor: Les Goldman
Animation: Ken Harris, Don Towsley, Tom Ray, Dick Thompson, Ben Washam
Story: John Dunn
Music: Eugene Poddany
Graphics Advisor: Maurice Noble
Set Design: Philip Deguard
Tracing: Don Morgan
Metrocolor (6 min. 46 sec.)

Space Station No. 1. Jerry grabs a piece of cheese. Tom is on alert. He sees Jerry on his television screen and immediately sends out his robot cat, but the robot cat pushes Tom instead of catching Jerry. Tom fires a laser beam at Jerry's hole, but the mouse surrounds it with smoke. Tom tears himself

apart trying to catch Jerry. He is soon sent flying in all directions by a jet engine. He chases after Jerry and ends up inside a ventilator, from which he emerges in tatters. Jerry winds up inside the cheese. Tom continues shooting with his space weapon and riddles the station with holes. Finally the space station is patched together again while Jerry lolls about inside a piece of cheese.

GUIDED MOUSE-ILLE

Director: Abe Levitow
Producer: Chuck Jones
(Metro-Goldwyn-Mayer)
Production Supervisor: Les Goldman
Animation: Don Towsley, Tom Ray, Dick Thompson, Ben Washam, Ken Harris, Philip Roman
Story: John Dunn
Music: Eugene Poddany
Set Design: Thelma Witmer
Tracing: Don Morgan
Graphics Advisor: Maurice Noble
Metrocolor (6 min. 45 sec.)

The year is 2565. Jerry uses a robot-mouse to steal some cheese. The robot-mouse blocks out a ray of light and Tom, alerted, sends a robot-cat after him. The robot-mouse comes out of Tom's monitor screen. So does the cat but he breaks everything around him. Tom spies Jerry eating cheese. He makes himself invisible, but Jerry makes him visible again and shoots him. The robot-cat, demolished by Jerry, draws on Tom. Jerry hits Tom with several blows of a club. Tom is completely squashed and flattened out. Jerry attacks Tom with a little bomb that goes off in a huge explosion. We're now back to prehistoric times. Tom and Jerry chew on the same bone before chasing after each other.

Notes

• The film's complete title is "Guided Mouse-ille or Science on a Wet Afternoon!"

• The robot-cat is the same as the character in "O-Solar Meow." The two films were obviously conceived at the same time.

ROCK 'N' RODENT

Director: Abe Levitow
Producer: Chuck Jones
(Metro-Goldwyn-Mayer)
Production Supervisor: Les Goldman
Animation: Ben Washam, Dick Thompson, Tom Ray, Don Towsley, Ken Harris
Story: Bob Ogle
Music: Carl Brandt
Graphics Advisor: Maurice Noble
Set Design: Philip Deguard
Tracing: Don Morgan
Metrocolor (6 min. 32 sec.)

Tom sets his alarm and goes to sleep. Jerry, on the other hand, wakes up, takes a shower in a leaking pipe, combs his hair, and goes to a nightclub. He plays drums in a rock band there. Tom is awakened by the music. He tries to stop the noise by flooding the cellar, but a big dog comes along and throws him out. Tom, trying to draw out what he takes to be the source of the noise with a suction pump, sucks in the dog's radio and gets thrown into his basket. Tom is exhausted. He wraps his head up to escape the noise. All is now silent, and Tom is finally content. Jerry goes to sleep and Tom is awakened by the alarm clock just as he is about to fall asleep. He screams and runs off right through the wall. Jerry, strutting like Chaplin, returns to his hole.

1967

CANNERY RODENT

Director: Chuck Jones
Producer: Chuck Jones
(Metro-Goldwyn-Mayer)
Production Supervisor: Les Goldman
Codirector: Maurice Noble
Animation: Ben Washam, Ken Harris,
Don Towsley, Tom Ray, Dick
Thompson, O.E. Barkley, Bob Kirk
Story: Chuck Jones
Production Director: Earl Jonas
Music: Dean Elliott
Coordinator: Sam Pal
Set Design: Philip Deguard
Camera Planning: Buf Nerbovig
Metrocolor (6 min. 28 sec.)

Tom is chasing Jerry. They soon find themselves in a canning factory, then inside cans of preserves. Tom gets out and falls into the water. He emerges, pale, pursued by a shark. He drops a heavy anchor on the shark. Jerry gets out of his can. Tom chases after him and falls into the water. The

shark rushes toward him. Tom hits him with an oar but the shark tries to swallow him. To save him, Jerry throws pepper in the shark's face, and he's blown into the canning factory and soon canned. Jerry appears, like an angel with a halo, and Tom like a devil with horns. Tom falls into the water and flees, pursued by Jerry who, using an artificial fin, makes Tom believe he's being chased by a real shark.

1965

THE MOUSE FROM H.U.N.G.E.R.

Director: Abe Levitow
Producer: Chuck Jones
(Metro-Goldwyn-Mayer)
Production Supervisor: Les Goldman
Animation: Philip Roman, Ben
Washam, Ken Harris, Don Towsley,
Tom Ray, Dick Thompson
Story: Bob Ogle
Music: Dean Elliott
Production Director: Earl Jonas
Drawings: Don Foster
Graphics Advisor: Maurice Noble
Set Design: Bob Inman
Tracing: Don Morgan
Metrocolor (6 min. 47 sec.)

Secret agent Jerry makes his way, after many detours, to headquarters. There he is present at the screening of a film that shows a castle filled with cheese, with Tom Thrush standing guard. He drives there in a convertible. Tom spots him and prepares various traps. Jerry is charmed by a voluptuous young mouse who blows up in his face. He continues on his way. Tom hides the amply filled refrigerator, placed in a strongbox, inside a giant television set. He lays mines and places barbed wire around to keep Jerry from approaching. He is enjoying in advance the result of these traps. Jerry arrives. Tom, hearing steps that have been previously recorded by Jerry, thinks he has entered and is caught in his own traps, which now begin to go off. Tom collapses and Jerry leaves with the refrigerator and its contents.

Note
• The title obviously refers to MGM's series, "The Man from U.N.C.L.E." Thrush was the name of the enemy organization in the series.

1967

SURF-BORED CAT

Director: Abe Levitow
Producer: Chuck Jones
(Metro-Goldwyn-Mayer)
Production Supervisor: Les Goldman
Animation: Dick Thompson, Philip
Roman, Ben Washam, Hal Ambro,
Don Towsley, Carl Bell
Story: Bob Ogle
Music: Dean Elliott
Production Director: Earl Jonas
Graphics Advisor: Maurice Noble
Set Design: Philip Deguard
Tracing: Don Morgan
Checker: Carole Barnes
Coordinator: Kathy Troxel
Metrocolor (6 min. 38 sec.)

A steamship arrives with Tom and Jerry on board. Tom intends to do some surfing, but he has a lot of trouble reaching the ocean. He finally gets there and attacks a threatening shark. He rides the surf but the shark is still there. The shark chases Tom, who is soon literally buried beneath the beach. He reappears with an octopus on his head. Tom tries to get rid of the octopus but its tentacles keep hold of him. Tom hits up against a rock and the octopus finally leaves. Jerry is surfing and dancing on the board. Tom is furious. He takes back his board, and Jerry's head is soon looking like a coconut. The shark swallows the board and Tom bursts into laughter. The shark coughs up

the board, and Tom swallows it. Jerry goes surfing using Tom as the board.

SHUTTER BUGGED CAT

Story, Direction, and Supervision:
Tom Ray
Producer: Metro-Goldwyn-Mayer
Continuity: Bob Ogle
Animation: Irven Spence, Ed Barge,
Ken Muse, George Gordon, Pete
Burgess, Lewis Marshall, Ray
Patterson
Direction: William Hanna, Joseph
Barbera
Music: Dean Elliott
Additional Sets: Philip Deguard
Sound Editing: Lovell Norman
Metrocolor (6 min. 48 sec.)

Tom is screening some old films. Tom,
with an ear of corn in his hand, catches
Jerry in the refrigerator.

Jerry sets some bottles of milk rolling. He
rolls a bowling ball over Tom's head. The
cat slips on the staircase railing and falls out
the window. Jerry throws some egg grenades at Tom, and sinks him with a subma-
rine grenade. He lights a stick of dynamite,
which explodes under Tom (sequences
from "The Yankee Doodle Mouse," 1943).

Jerry, meanwhile, has also come out of
his hole with a package of popcorn, to see
the screening. Tom pulls on the staircase
carpet to make Jerry fall, but he is crushed
by the piano (sequence from "Heavenly
Puss," 1949).

Tom runs the film backward, then forward again. He tries different approaches.
He pursues Jerry, but the mouse eludes him
and he knocks his head against the wall.

Tom designs a sophisticated trap with
which to catch Jerry. The mouse, passing
through a clever mechanism, should finally
be crushed by the fall of a strongbox; but
Jerry changes just one number and it's Tom,
not the mouse, who is crushed by the safe
(sequence from "Designs on Jerry," 1955).
Tom, covered with bandages and furious,
tears up the plan of his trap.

Note
• **The film includes extracts from "The Yankee Doodle
Mouse" (1943), "Heavenly Puss" (1949), and "Designs on
Jerry" (1955).**

ADVANCE AND BE MECHANIZED

Director: Ben Washam
Producer: Chuck Jones
(Metro-Goldwyn-Mayer)
Production Supervisor: Les Goldman
Animation: Dick Thompson, Ben
Washam, Don Towsley, Philip Roman
Story: Bob Ogle
Music: Dean Elliott
Coordinator: Nick Iuppa
Graphics Advisor: Maurice Noble
Set Design: Philip Deguard
Tracing: Don Morgan
Director of Production: Earl Jonas
Metrocolor (6 min. 33 sec.)

In the world of tomorrow the universe is
populated by robots. Jerry sends a robot-
mouse to steal some cheese. Tom, who
heads police control, spots the robot-mouse
and sends a robot-cat after him. The robot-
cat tears the robot-mouse to bits. Tom
laughs, but he's sick of the robot food he's
been getting. He wants to eat Jerry. He sees
the robot-mouse and sends his cat out once
again. The robot-cat bumps into a wall.
Crippled, the robot-cat changes Tom into
a robot while the robot-mouse, also
wounded, sends Jerry, who's also a robot
now. Robot-Tom faces Robot-Jerry and they
go at one another.

PURR-CHANCE TO DREAM

Director: Ben Washam
Producer: Chuck Jones
(Metro-Goldwyn-Mayer)
Production Supervisor: Les Goldman
Animation: Dick Thompson, Ken
Harris, Don Towsley, Tom Ray,
Philip Roman
Story: Irv Spector
Music: Carl Brandt
Director of Production: Earl Jonas
Graphics Advisor: Maurice Noble
Set Design: Philip Deguard
Tracing: Don Morgan
Graphics: Don Foster
Metrocolor (6 min. 5 sec.)

Tom is chasing Jerry when he runs into a
gigantic dog who attacks him. Tom
wakes up; it was only a terrible nightmare.
Jerry comes in with a bone and hides inside
the dog's corner. It's a tiny dog. Tom starts
to laugh and grabs Jerry, but the little dog

attacks him and makes mincemeat of him.
Then he frees Jerry. The mouse then feeds
the puppy. Tom sprinkles himself with "re-
pellent" scent. This drives the dog away and
Tom is able to make a sandwich of Jerry.
Tom is now torn to pieces by the dog. He
tries to get rid of him but the little dog re-
duces Tom to a heap of hair.

Tom shuts the dog up in a safe and buries
it. But the little dog escapes and once again
makes mincemeat of Tom. Tom finally falls
asleep with the help of some sleeping pills.

186

190

19

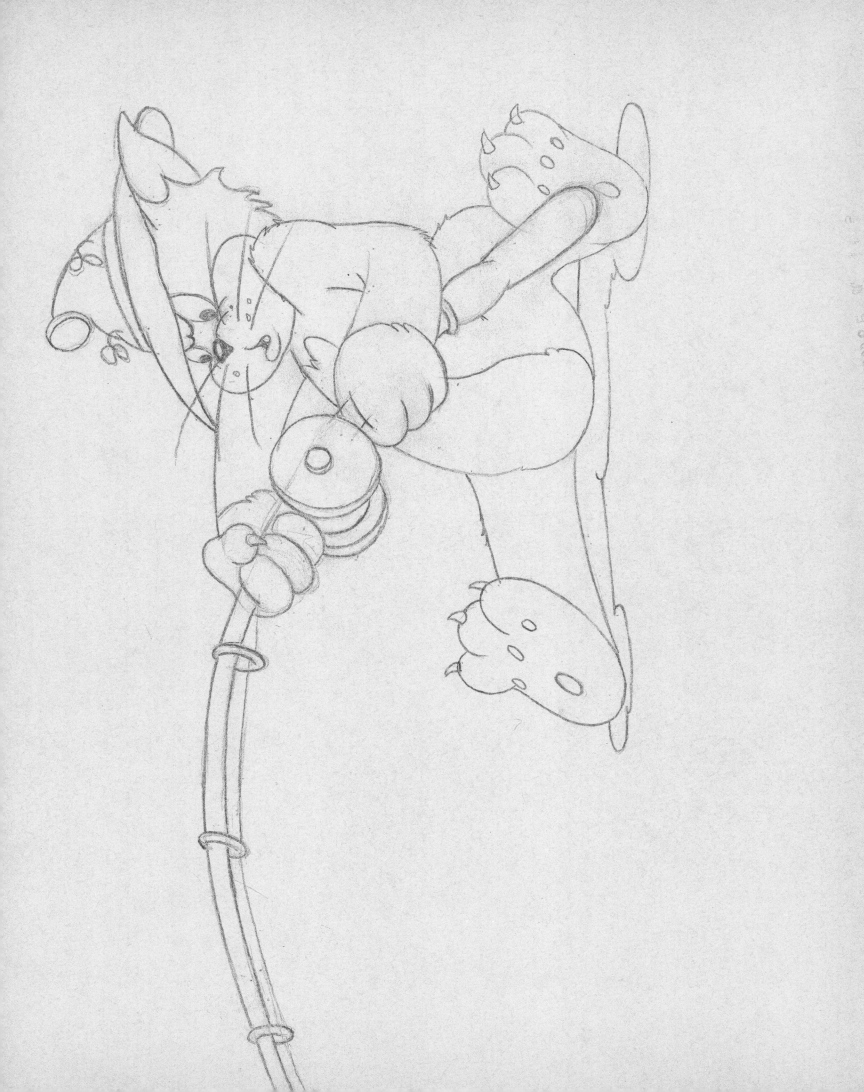

PROD 1 82 SC 30

BS 2 60 "R

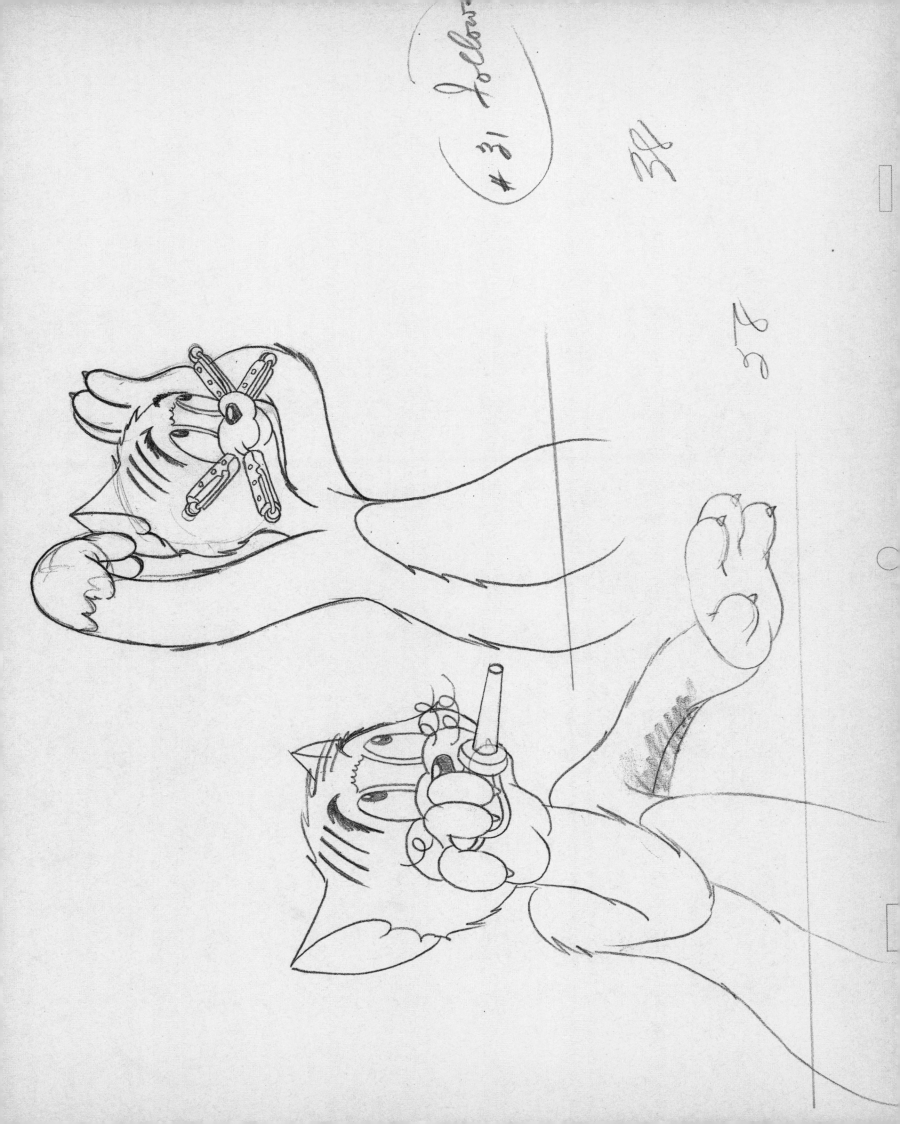

Paint BACKGROUND (LIGHTS ON)
NORMAL WILL
CAMERA EXPOSE
UNDER DARKNESS
FOR DARKNESS

BYE LEVEL

Prod #297

Sc. 26

FIELDS

SC. NO 3.   16
M   16
CHECK   ✓   DIR ✓

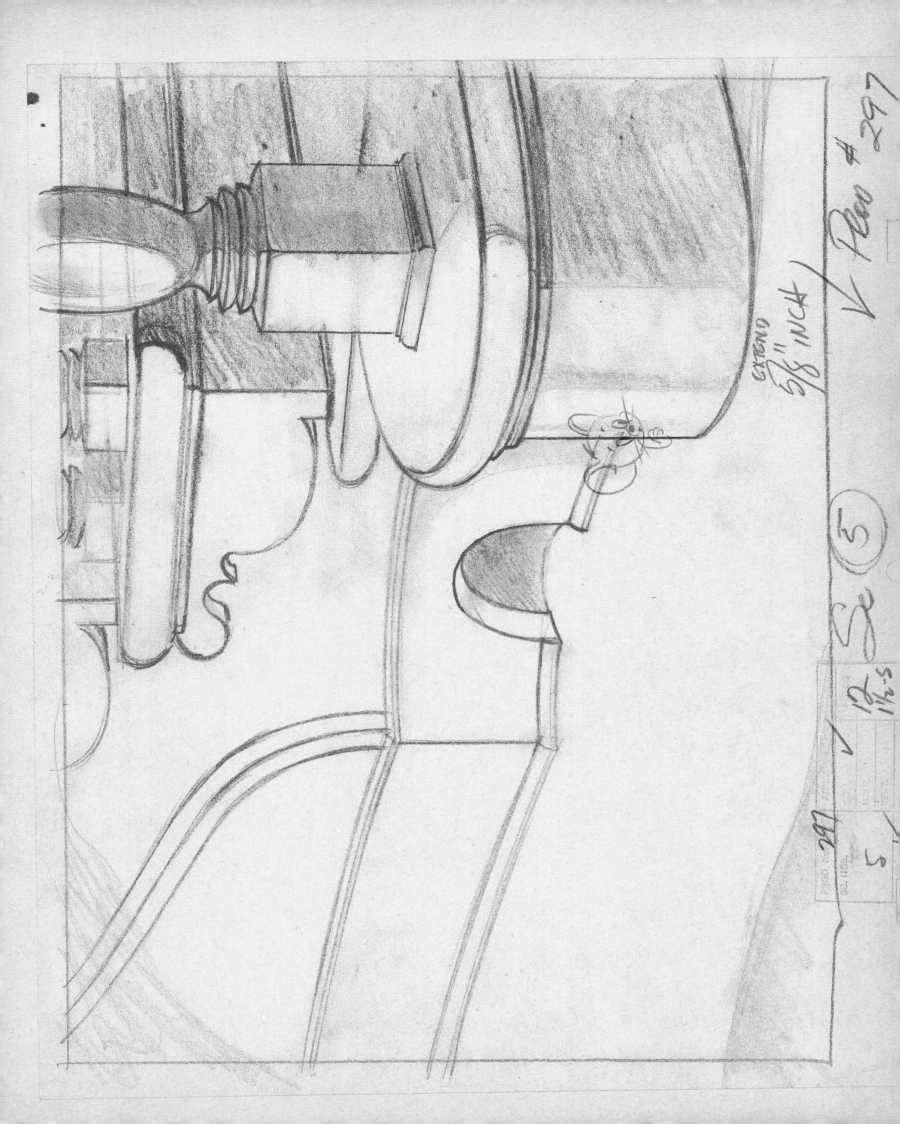

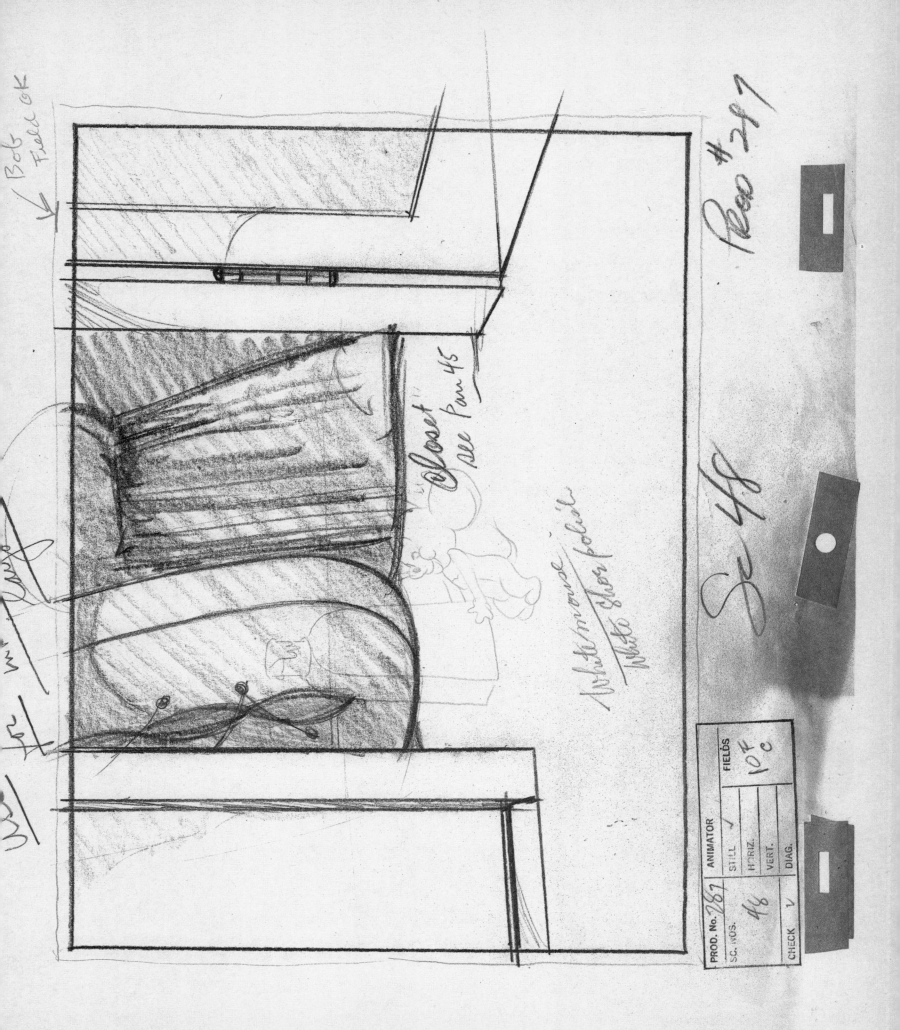

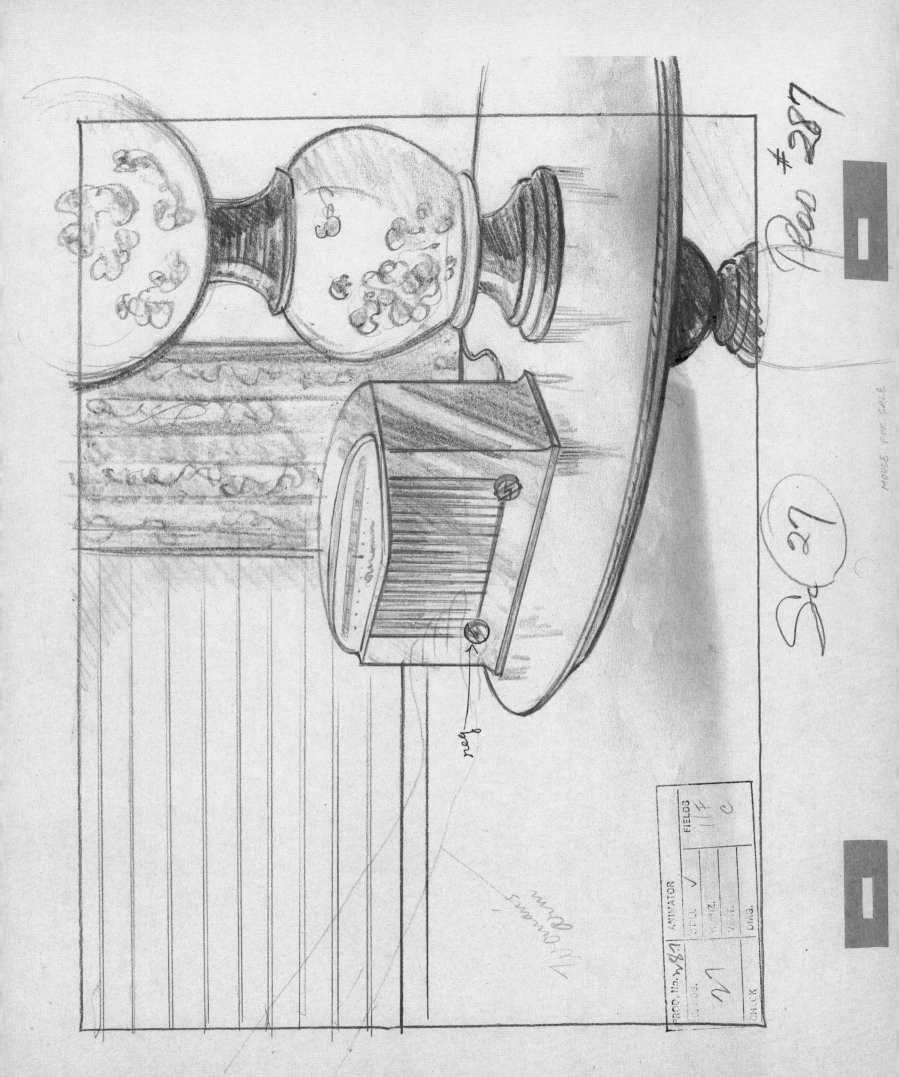

INDEX OF FILMS

BIBLIOGRAPHY

Books:

Maltin, Leonard. *Of Mice and Magic.* (New York: New American Library, 1980).

Lenburg, Jeff. *The Great Cartoon Directors.* (Jefferson, N.C.: McFarland, 1983).

———. *The Encyclopedia of Animated Cartoon Series.* (Westport, Conn.: Arlington House, 1981).

Friedwald, Will, and Jerry Beck. *The Warner Brothers Cartoons.* (Metuchen, New Jersey: Scarecrow Press, 1981).

Adamson, Joe. *Tex Avery: King of Cartoons.* (New York: Popular Library, 1975).

Articles:

Lenne, Gérard. "Tom and Jerry," in *La Revue du Cinema,* no. 424, February 1987.

Mayerson, Mark. "The Lion Began with a Frog," in *The Velvet Light Trap,* no. 18, Spring 1978.

Kausler, Mark. "Tom and Jerry," in *Film Comment,* January–February 1975; "William Hanna," in *Film Dope,* no. 23, September 1981; "Joseph Barbera," in *Film Dope,* no. 2, March 1973; and "Chuck Jones," in *Film Dope,* no. 28, December 1983.

Quimby, Fred. "The Cartoon Story," in *The Hollywood Reporter,* October 29, 1951.

Benayoun, Robert. "Cinq jours avec Chuck Jones," in *Positif,* no. 54–55, July–August 1963.